Confidence in a Changing Church

✧

And the Church must be forever building, and always decaying, and always being restored.

T. S. Eliot, Choruses from *The Rock*, 1934, II

✧

FINLAY A. J. MACDONALD

SAINT ANDREW PRESS
Edinburgh

First published in 2004 by
SAINT ANDREW PRESS
121 George Street, Edinburgh EH2 4YN

Copyright © Finlay A. J. Macdonald, 2004

ISBN 0 7152 0812 8

The right of Finlay A. J. Macdonald to be identified as author of this work has been asserted in
accordance with the Copyright, Designs and Patents Act 1988.

British Library Cataloguing in Publication Date
A catalogue record for this book
is available from the British Library

Typeset by Waverley Typesetters, Galashiels
Printed and bound by Bell & Bain Ltd, Glasgow

Confidence in a Changing Church

Contents

Foreword

This is an important book, able to fulfil a number of functions. It is about a Church but it is also about a country and its history. Part of it centres on a single year – its author's year as Moderator – but it covers a sweep of centuries. The focus of its subject-matter is held to be eternal, yet it is about change.

Finlay Macdonald is a scholar. Having started by studying law at university, he graduated with a degree in philosophy and went on to study theology before spending twenty-five years in the parish ministry. In 1983 he was awarded a Ph.D. from St Andrews for a thesis which explored the constitutional significance of the Westminster Confession of Faith for the Church of Scotland. Since 1996 he has been Principal Clerk to the General Assembly of the Church of Scotland, and in 2002 he served as Moderator of the General Assembly. These solemn facts belie the warmth and wit of the book's author. Finlay Macdonald's sense of proportion is illuminated by a ready sense of humour. He is a historian, and his personal history draws on Scotland's Gaelic heritage, for his father was a native of the Isle of Lewis. He is also a gifted and knowledgeable musician, a pianist and organist with a particular interest in sacred music. His appreciation of Scotland, while its chief focus is in the Church, embraces an enjoyment of the countryside and especially of the hills where with his family he has always loved to walk.

After working as a parish minister in Clackmannanshire and in Glasgow Finlay Macdonald was appointed Principal Clerk. The Principal Clerk of the General Assembly of the Church of Scotland is positioned at the centre of the Church's complex organisation of committees, and has the opportunity to observe and to some degree influence their interaction. A Principal Clerk's reflections, therefore, will be of immense interest to anyone concerned with the life and role of the Church of Scotland. Until now no Principal Clerk has committed to print anything other than expositions of the law of the Church, and Finlay Macdonald's own preferred way of working was to remain firmly out of sight, 'below the parapet' as he might say. When he was elected Moderator of the General Assembly he was required to take a higher public profile, and when that year of office came to an end he was evidently ready to offer comment and observation more publicly than before.

As became familiar to me when I was Moderator of the General Assembly in 2001 the Principal Clerk's office is lined with glass-fronted book-cases, their shelves full of specially bound volumes. These are the Minutes of the Assemblies of the family of Presbyterian churches whose traditions have formed what is now the Church of Scotland. I found that Finlay Macdonald's knowledge of the history of the church and of how it had dealt with matters in the past was always helpful in deciding how to address the present. He has an ability to harmonise sometimes discordant notes, and to ensure that disparate issues can be addressed with integrity.

Confidence in a Changing Church epitomises his capacity to enable current events and issues to be informed by a sense of history. I recall thinking that in his function as Principal Clerk Finlay Macdonald's role was like that of an editor of the Church of Scotland's life. The job of an editor is to ensure so far as possible a harmony of styles and a consistency of direction across a wide range of material. This often seemed to me the essence of his own work, as he continually found ways to include different events as part of the pattern of the life of the Church. That skilled hand is at work in these pages. To the extent that Finlay Macdonald can be seen as having an editorial role in respect of the public face of the Church of Scotland, we may see this book as his editorial. The book has been awaited with particular anticipation.

To committed Christians who have a live engagement with the Church of Scotland it will be of exceptional interest. Indeed such readers will find their understanding of the Church's operation greatly enhanced, and even those who have spent a life-time in the Church will learn much about its history. But the book does more than address merely the constituency of the Church's own membership. Small in size but large in scope, the book will be a valuable resource to anyone who has a serious interest in Scotland's life and character. For the author has woven together Church history and many developments in Scotland's political life, themes of theology and doctrine, the intricacies of Church procedures, the role of Presbyterianism at home and abroad over the centuries, the encounter between the historic Christian faith and the ever-changing culture, and the increasingly significant relationships between Christianity and other world faiths.

In spite of huge and accelerating cultural change the role of the churches remains significant in today's world. In 2001, within days of the 11 September terrorist attacks in the United States, the British Prime Minister Mr Blair called the leaders of Britain's faith communities to Downing Street. Christian, Jewish, Muslim, Hindu, Buddhist and other religious leaders were invited to consider how their respective communities could work together to minimise the tensions and antagonisms which might follow the acts of terror. That government-sponsored assembly was an acknowledgement that faith reaches deeper into the basis of society than perhaps any other constituent of communal life. No-one can study the history of Britain without studying the role of Christianity and the Church, and no-one can address the issues which face Britain today without taking account of the churches. Similarly, anyone who wishes to understand today's Scotland must weigh the role of the churches, and among them the Church of Scotland.

Confidence in a Changing Church is published at a time when people's interest in spiritual matters is as great as ever it was, but when the historic churches are failing to offer their spiritual truths in an accessible form. Finlay Macdonald's book recalls to people's minds the deep roots of the Church's faith in God, and sets out evidence of its continuing relevance to the society of today.

Within the space of two years Saint Andrew Press has published two books about the Church of Scotland. In respect of their relationship with the Church the two authors could scarcely be more different: the one a journalist and an avowed outsider, the other the epitome of the insider, a mandarin, the church's most senior bureaucrat. Harry Reid's book, *Outside Verdict*, published in 2002, raised the profile of many contentious issues and gave rise to widespread discussion within the Church and beyond. Being written, however, from the standpoint of an albeit sympathetic outsider, Reid's book could not but be superficial in its treatment of much of the detail of the Church's life. By contrast, Finlay Macdonald's *Confidence in a Changing Church* is substantially grounded in the day-to-day issues which arise in the life of Scotland's parishes and committees. Accordingly it seeks to point to what is of lasting value in the traditions which it embodies. It will undoubtedly be an important contribution to the debate about the future shape of the Church.

The Reverend John Miller

Introduction

The idea of writing this book was formed during the course of my Moderatorial year.

A question commonly asked of Moderators in waiting is whether they have a theme for the year. I thought about this and, while anxious not to have a controlling agenda, certainly saw value in having some underlying objectives which might bring coherence to a miscellany of engagements and events. I reflected that Moderators are called upon to communicate, both internally to the Church and externally to the wider community and world. Having regard to the latter I judged that inter-faith relations would be a timely subject; for an internal theme I came up with the phrase, 'Faith in the Gospel and Confidence in the Church'.

Church without Walls has reminded us that, essentially, being a member of the Church involves not so much belonging to an institution as being a disciple of Jesus Christ. I agree. In turn, being a disciple of Jesus Christ involves a call to have faith in the Gospel and live our lives by it. But, if it is self-evident that Church members are people who profess faith in the Gospel, what about confidence in the Church? Surely, if we believe in Christ and recognise that the Church is his body in the world, then faith in the Gospel ought to be complemented by confidence in the Church. The truth is rather different. Dreary litanies of declining membership, loss of influence, decaying buildings and financial problems have inexorably undermined morale and sapped the Church's self-confidence. Indeed, it appears sometimes that the gloomiest predictions of imminent extinction come from within the Church itself!

1

Reflecting on this, my task seemed clear. As I travelled within the Church, visiting presbyteries, congregations and other groups, I should seek to raise morale and build up a sense, not only of faith in the Gospel, but also of confidence in the Church. On more than one occasion I found myself quoting a remark of Eleanor Roosevelt: 'No-one can make you feel inferior without your consent.'

One reason for writing this book, therefore, was to offer an account which shows how, over the past half-century or so, the Church of Scotland, far from being stuck in the past, has developed and evolved in a variety of ways. The various chapter headings indicate the range of areas covered. Of course there have been disagreements and divisions along the way. I do not for one moment suggest that the Church has enthusiastically embraced every fresh idea or unanimously heeded every prophetic challenge. In the chapters which follow there is plenty of evidence of 'foot-dragging'. My call is for confidence in the Church, not self-satisfied complacency. At the same time, I believe that these chapters also show that, under the Gospel and the promised renewal of the Holy Spirit, the Church of Scotland has changed and continues to do so, the better to minister to the people of Scotland and the wider world beyond. I believe, therefore, that we can take a certain pride and confidence in what has been achieved.

The second reason for offering this book at this particular time is to provide some recent background to the current debate over change within the Church. Like many public bodies the Church is subject to a continuing process of review and assessment. Recent years have witnessed a bewildering raft of initiatives touching on virtually every aspect of Church life. Sometimes, it has to be said, these have been presented in ways which suggest that even a moment's hesitation in signing up will mean the disappearance of the Church of Scotland overnight. The fact is, however, that change is of the essence of the Gospel and it would, indeed, be ironic were the Church to be the one body excluded from its Lord's promise to make all things new. Not all change, of course, is necessarily for the better and it is simply not true, as is sometimes implied, that the Church's structures and procedures inhibit change. I have always understood the purpose of procedures as being to facilitate things being done decently and in order, not to obstruct new things the Church is minded to do. It is critical that there should be openness within the Church and not an automatic resistance to change. The classic joke about the old beadle advising his successor to 'resist all improvements' is no longer funny. The Gamaliel principle (see Acts 5) still applies. If something is of God it will succeed. I am confident that much of the energy being directed at the present time to change within the Church is of God and will therefore be a blessing to his people. However, we should never be so arrogant as to think of ourselves as the only generation called to be change-bearing. This book can help us see how our present energies are but an entering into the change-inducing efforts of those who have gone before.

My third reason for writing this book is to fill what I perceive to be something of a gap. Two of my predecessors as Principal Clerk to the General Assembly, James Cox and James Weatherhead, have written classic volumes on the Kirk's law, constitution, practice and procedure. Another famous Clerk, the late Andrew Herron of Glasgow Presbytery, also produced a most useful resource in his *Law and Practice of the Kirk*. These learned texts provide an invaluable repository of specialist knowledge for those who have to manage the Kirk's business at congregational, presbytery and national levels. However, Clerks, as well has having responsibilities in matters of practice and procedure, also have a rather privileged overview of the life of the Court and Church which they serve. I have therefore chosen to write something more general and seek to provide elders, ministers, Church members and others interested in Church matters, with an account of some of the big issues which have faced the Church of Scotland over the course of my own ministry. My hope is that it will enable people to feel better informed about the Church to which they belong.

While the book has been written as a connected narrative, each chapter can stand on its own. I have adopted a practical, 'hands-on' approach to the material. Inevitably, however, there are some variations in style dictated by the subject matter. For example, the chapter on inter-faith relations offers a personal account of meetings and encounters, mainly during the course of my Moderatorial year. By contrast, the chapter on doctrine is quite 'heavy' in terms of theological and constitutional content. It deals, principally, with the relationship between the Church of Scotland and the Westminster Confession of Faith, a seventeenth-century document referred to in services of ordination as the Church's 'subordinate standard', even though it is largely unfamiliar to elders and the Church's membership as a whole.

I conclude these introductory comments with some acknowledgements. While, as I have said, the idea of writing this book came to me during the Moderatorial year, it might well have remained 'all talk' were it not for the gentle but firm encouragement of my wife, Elma. As ever, I am grateful for that. One of the great blessings I experienced on coming to work in 121 George Street was the friendship of colleagues who were all around me. Despite what some may think, we do talk to each other and try to work together as a team in the service of the whole Church. I am particularly grateful to John Chalmers, Douglas Galbraith, Sheilagh Kesting, Marjory MacLean and Kenneth Ross for casting an eye over chapters relating to their particular spheres of expertise and making helpful suggestions. I have incorporated many of these with gratitude. At the same time I make clear that responsibility for the final text, including any remaining errors, is mine and mine alone. In addition, I record my thanks to Alison Murray for kindly undertaking the detailed work involved in obtaining the necessary permissions to quote material from published sources.

Finally, I am enormously grateful to Ann Crawford of Saint Andrew Press. Her enthusiastic response to my proposal provided a great source of energy and her wise suggestions as the work proceeded have greatly improved the finished article.

Finlay A. J. Macdonald

1

The Nature of the Church of Scotland

ORIGINS AND DEVELOPMENT

There is a popular misconception that the Church of Scotland began in 1560, the year of the Scottish Reformation. This view gains credence from newspaper reports and the like, which commonly use phrases such as 'the Kirk's five-hundred-year history'. This notion is quite wrong and its correction is fundamental to a proper understanding of the nature of the Church of Scotland today.

There are different chapters in the history of Scottish Church life.

The earliest beginnings were associated with names like Ninian at Whithorn (late fourth century) and Columba of Iona (mid-sixth century). Many church dedications throughout the country maintain the memory of local saints from this period – Ninian, Columba, Mungo, Serf, Kane, Fillan, Quivox – and connect the modern Church of Scotland to these earliest days. G. D. Henderson in his *Claims of the Church of Scotland* is quite clear: 'The history of the Church of Scotland goes back to St Ninian.'[1]

Gradually Scottish Christianity and Church life came into greater conformity with the life of the medieval western church. Names associated with this period are the saintly Queen Margaret (eleventh century) and her son, King David I. On account of the latter's generosity in endowing abbeys and erecting cathedrals he became known as 'a sair saint for the Crown'. The legacy of these days can be seen in the great ecclesiastical ruins of Melrose, Jedburgh, Dryburgh, St Andrews and Elgin and in restored and living cathedral churches such as Glasgow Cathedral, Edinburgh's St Giles', Aberdeen's St Machar's,

Dunblane, Dunkeld, Dornoch and St Magnus in Kirkwall. Indeed these pre-Reformation buildings happily and comfortably accommodate congregations of the Kirk today. This period is also part of the history of the Church of Scotland.

In the first half of the sixteenth century the Reformation movement, associated with names like Martin Luther and John Calvin, gained influence in Scotland and was officially embraced by the Scottish Parliament in August 1560. Like their continental counterparts, those who led the Scottish Reformation were quite clear that they were not starting a new church but reforming an old one. To quote Henderson again:

> Scots, like other Christians would claim that the development . . . was a true evolution and that the Reformation had cleared away accretions and restored genuine identity and characteristic continuity, so that in spite of many differences the essential oneness has been preserved.[2]

In similar vein J. T. Cox in his *Practice and Procedure in the Church of Scotland* speaks of the Reformation as 'a new chapter, perhaps rather a new volume' in the chronicles of the Church and is quite emphatic that 'it was not a new church which suddenly sprang into being'. Cox continues:

> That achievement [the Reformation] was not [the Church's] origin but its re-formation, while in great measure also its transformation, without loss of its identity. The Church of our fathers [sic] has a much longer lineage and a much greater heritage than is comprised in four centuries. It has been built up, stage by stage, 'upon the foundation of the apostles and prophets, Jesus Christ Himself being the chief corner-stone'. The Church of Scotland is a part of the One Holy and Catholic Church.[3]

Henderson points out that an important reason for this sense of continuity was that the Church was not identified with the clergy 'but with the living Christian community as the body of Christ'.[4] This is a crucial point and one to which we shall return. It also ties in with a powerful political theme which runs throughout Scottish history, namely, that political sovereignty lies ultimately with the people.

The years following the Reformation were turbulent ones, frequently characterised by an excess of zeal and short supplies of grace. Throughout the seventeenth century the reformed Church of Scotland endured a power struggle between two forms of ecclesiastical government – Episcopalianism and Presbyterianism. The Stuart kings (James VI and I, Charles I and Charles II) sought to control the Church through bishops and, after all, the Church of England had managed to embrace the protestant Reformation and retain episcopal government. However, owing largely to the influence of Andrew Melville and *The Second Book of Discipline* of 1578, to which he was a significant contributor, Presbyteriansim, with its conciliar rather than personal hierarchy, had taken a hold in the hearts of many. Eventually, the issue was resolved following the 1688 revolution which banished James VII and II and brought William and Mary to the throne. In 1690 the Church of Scotland was 'by law established' as a presbyterian church and, in 1712, the Act of Toleration gave legal recognition to a separate Scottish Episcopal Church.[5]

By its very nature Presbyterianism is a participatory form of church government, with ready made channels for the people to express their views. The authority of Christ as King and Head of the Church is vested in the courts of the Church and not in any one individual. The discernment of Christ's will for the Church relies on a process which involves debate, within the context of prayer for the guidance of the Holy Spirit. Presbyterianism is also strong on the right of conscience with a consequent reluctance to compel individuals to go against deeply held principles. All of this, when put together, can lead, and frequently does, to fragmentation and division.

So it was throughout the eighteenth and early nineteenth centuries. In 1733 and 1761 two groups broke away, or were driven out, from the established church. The first of these secessions, led by Ebenezer Erskine, had to do largely with the freedom of congregations to call their own ministers, rather than simply accept the patron's appointee. The second secession, associated with the name of Thomas Gillespie, led to the foundation of the Relief Church which, as the name suggests, offered a haven for those who felt their consciences were being oppressed. T. M. Devine in *The Scottish Nation 1700–2000* describes some of those who left in the first secession as 'of rigidly puritanical inclination' and remarks that 'their departure made it easier for more liberal opinion to become influential in the General Assembly'. Given such a mindset it is hardly surprising that by the end of the century these seceders had fragmented into four warring groups over the question of Church–State relations, focused on the Burgess Oath,[6] and also over the emergence of new theological ideas (old light and new light). Old light burghers, new light burghers, old light anti-burghers and new light anti-burghers cheerfully anathematised one another and not only congregations, but families, were split apart. By contrast Devine describes the second secession as 'much more important' on the grounds that

> this not only attracted much greater numbers than the Associate Presbytery [the original seceders], but also offered a more liberal alternative to the Established Church. The Relief Church, for instance, imposed no doctrinal requirements on those who wished to attend communion.[7]

The practice of inviting to the Lord's Table members of any branch of the Christian Church is part of Gillespie's legacy to the contemporary Church of Scotland. In all of this we can see the seeds of tensions which exist within today's Church over issues which would have been unimaginable to our eighteenth-century forebears such as inter-faith relations and human sexuality – of which more, in due course.

By far the greatest schism within the Presbyterian establishment was the Disruption of 1843. The vexed issue of the right of the people to choose their own ministers had rumbled on since the days of Erskine and was no nearer a resolution. The Church's freedom to manage its own affairs was also seriously challenged over two pieces of legislation enacted by the General Assembly. These were the Veto and Chapels Acts of 1834. The former sought to give male heads of families a right of veto over the patron's nominee for a vacant parish. The latter claimed the right to establish new ecclesiastical parishes, with Kirk Sessions, and their ministers having seats in Church courts. Both of these Acts of Assembly were held by the civil courts to be beyond the power of the General Assembly. Faced with these challenges to its authority and the unwillingness of the civil government to intervene, the stage was set for the great Disruption in which approximately one-third of the ministers of the Church of Scotland left the security of their charges and manses and, under the leadership of Thomas Chalmers, formed the Free Church. Robin Jenkins's novel *The Awakening of George Darroch* gives dramatic expression to this momentous, though increasingly unremembered, event. Indeed, in a foreword to the novel Jenkins deplores the fact that a book giving a year-by-year account of 'events of consequence' recently consulted by him had recorded under 1843 the first publication of the *News of the World* but had not even mentioned the Disruption![8]

However, even as the Presbyterian establishment was being further fractured, processes of healing and reconciliation were underway. In 1820 the new light burghers and anti-burghers had come together to form the United Secession Church and this, in turn, joined with the Relief Church in 1847 to form the United Presbyterian Church. In 1900 the United Presbyterian Church joined with the overwhelming majority of the Free Church to form the United Free Church, which, in turn joined with the Church of Scotland in 1929. Some had stayed out of these unions of 1900 and 1929 and continue today as the Free Church ('Wee Frees') and the United Free Church respectively. The Free Presbyterian Church dates from an 1893 secession from the Free Church, with the Associated Presbyterian Churches (APC) breaking away from the Free Presbyterian Church in 1989.

By 1929 the old causes of division had been largely resolved. Congregations were free to call ministers of their own choosing and the spiritual independence of the Church from the State had been guaranteed, though some within the United Free Church remained unconvinced. The particular genius of the 1929 union was encapsulated in the Declaratory Articles adopted by the General Assemblies of both uniting churches and appended to the Church of Scotland Act, 1921. These provided for both the national recognition of religion and the spiritual independence of the Church. The united Church was to be 'a national church' (Article III) but would exercise 'the right and power, subject to no civil authority, to legislate, and to adjudicate finally, in all matters of doctrine, worship, government and discipline in the Church . . .' (Article IV). Moreover, the Church's spiritual independence

9

was understood, not as something which Parliament had given but, rather, as something which it recognised. At the same time the 1921 Act declared: 'Nothing in this Act or in any other Act affecting the Church of Scotland shall prejudice the recognition of any other Church in Scotland as a Christian Church protected by law in the exercise of its spiritual function.'[9] Though possessing a unique status in terms of legal recognition of its independent spiritual jurisdiction, the twentieth-century Church of Scotland was to be one church among others within the life of the nation.

The fact is that, at the beginning of the twenty-first century, Scottish Church life finds expression in a variety of denominations – Church of Scotland, Roman Catholic, Scottish Episcopal, Methodist, Baptist, United Reformed Church, Society of Friends, Salvation Army, Pentecostalist, Orthodox, the various Presbyterian denominations already mentioned and others. Most of the 'mainline' churches work together through the ecumenical body Action of Churches Together in Scotland (ACTS). The Evangelical Alliance facilitates cooperation among a number of 'evangelical' churches. The Church of Scotland is a major player in ACTS as well as the United Kingdom and Ireland ecumenical body, Churches Together in Britain and Ireland (CTBI). In this context it is worth noting that, even, in the midst of the religious and political turmoil of the late sixteenth century, the framers of the *Second Book of Discipline* had an ecumenical vision of an Assembly of the 'haill [whole] Kirk of God'.[10] It is also relevant to mention that Article VII of the Declaratory Articles declares:

> The Church of Scotland, believing it to be the will of Christ that His disciples should be all one in the Father and in Him, that the world may believe that the Father has sent Him, recognises the obligation to seek and promote union with other Churches in which it finds the Word to be purely preached, the sacraments administered according to Christ's ordinance and discipline rightly exercised; and it has the right to unite with any such Church without loss of its identity on terms which this Church finds to be consistent with these Articles.

This sense of continuity and identity through change remains fundamental to the self-understanding of the present-day Church of Scotland.

Let me illustrate. In February 2002 I was a guest at the installation of the Most Reverend Mario Conti as Archbishop of Glasgow in the city's St Andrew's Roman Catholic Cathedral. It was a fine occasion at which, along with other ecumenical guests, I was made most warmly welcome. I noted that in the course of the service reference was made to the new archbishop as the successor of St Mungo, the sixth-century Bishop of Glasgow. As I heard this I thought of a plaque, in the sacristy of Glasgow Cathedral, which commemorates former ministers of the cathedral. The most recent name is that of the last minister Nevile Davidson (minister from 1935 to 1967). As the list goes back through the centuries the names of Presbyterian ministers merge into those of Protestant archbishops. As we continue through and beyond the Reformation we work through the names of long-forgotten medieval bishops, eventually reaching the first name on the long list – St Mungo whose tomb lies close by. Who then, today, is true successor of St Mungo? Is it the Roman Catholic Archbishop of Glasgow, or is it the Church of Scotland minister of Glasgow Cathedral? I suggest that the answer is that both are, and not just they but all who share in the Scottish Christian heritage. But the 'time travel' doesn't stop with St Mungo or even St Ninian. The Kirk's inheritance goes back, as does the heritage of all Christian people, to the apostles and prophets, Jesus Christ himself being the chief corner-stone. As Dr Cox has reminded us, 'The Church of Scotland is a part of the One Holy and Catholic Church.'

ESSENTIALS OF PRESBYTERIANISM

The Church of Scotland has been a Presbyterian church continuously since 1690. As already noted, this form of church government emerged in the aftermath of the sixteenth-century Reformation, finding its developed expression in the 1581 *Second Book of Discipline*. In essence, Presbyterianism provides for the government of the Church by an ascending series of courts. Already by 1560 the local Kirk Session, provincial synod and national General Assembly were in place. Alongside these was a gathering of ministers for prayer and Bible study which became known as 'the exercise'. Within twenty years this had evolved into the presbytery. So the familiar four-court pattern was established and this continued until the abolition of synods in 1992.

Over the years the courts of the Church have been modified, both in composition and in function. For example, in the eighteenth century Kirk Sessions would have had responsibilities for administering poor relief and overseeing the local school. The first General Assembly which met in December 1560 had forty-one members of whom six were ministers, the remainder being lairds and representatives of towns[11] – a very different body from the one we know today. Since 1966 women have been eligible for the eldership on the same terms and conditions as men, and the General Assembly of 1991 took a firm line in face of those who were wrongly treating this provision as merely permissive.

It has been said that Presbyterianism involves the government of the few by the many, rather than the many by the few. This reflects the description, noted in *Church without Walls*, of Presbyterianism as 'institutionalised distrust'.[12] Certainly the system can be cumbersome with plenty of scope for 'passing the buck' and slowing down the decision-making process. A presbytery meeting can easily become a 'talking shop' with decisions deferred 'pending further consideration', matters 'remitted back to the Committee', or 'further conference with the relevant Assembly Board'. Such phrases will sound wearily familiar to seasoned presbytery goers! Most frustrating of all for many church members is the length of time it can take to fill vacant charges, with seemingly endless negotiations over appraisal and readjustment before the actual search gets under way.

It is easy to offer such caricatures, though I suggest that they have more to do with the ways in which we have allowed the system to develop than with the system itself. Increasingly, as in the new vacancy procedures approved by the General Assembly of 2003, responsibility to 'get on with the job' is being entrusted to small groups within the presbytery, like the new Vacancy Procedures Committees, with business coming back to the whole presbytery only if there is a difficulty. One of the visions of the Group which produced the 2001 report 'Tomorrow's Presbyteries' was that, in the interests of informed and expeditious decision-making, more business should be delegated to groups within the presbytery. In effect the Group was saying that a culture of 'institutionalised *trust*' should be encouraged. At the beginning of 2004 the presbyteries of South Argyll, Dunoon and Lorn and Mull united to form the Presbytery of Argyll. The bounds of the new presbytery are extensive, with geography rendering the practical distance between two points anything but a straight line. The planned pattern is that the presbytery as a whole will meet four times a year with powers given to smaller, more locally based groups to carry the work forward between meetings. It is good to know that after all these centuries the system is capable of refreshment and renewal.

By its very nature the conciliar system makes for participatory government. At Kirk Session level elders, drawn from, and in many cases elected by the members, share with the minister in managing the congregation's affairs. Where financial matters are looked after by a congregational board or equivalent, members can be elected to serve without the additional commitment of the eldership. Such a democratic approach is healthy and, again, kept under review. For example, it has become increasingly difficult to draw hard-and-fast lines between 'matters spiritual' and 'matters temporal'. The Christian use of money is a highly spiritual question as is our stewardship of buildings. I welcome therefore the new unitary constitution which provides for the administration of a congregation's affairs by a single body, something which *quoad omnia*[13] churches never abandoned.

I am also of the opinion that elders should rotate their active membership of the Session having 'break years'. While we may politely applaud those who have given decades of service to specific offices within the Church (and there is no denying the depth of their dedication and the generosity of their service) change brings vital refreshment and renewal, something many Kirk Sessions lack. I am not impressed by the argument that people stay on because nobody else is prepared to take their place. The reality is quite the reverse. Nobody comes to take over because it is made subtly (and sometimes not so subtly!) clear that they are not welcome. If we genuinely believe in a form of government which is participatory then we need to encourage participation.

At the presbytery level more formal arrangements usually apply, with fixed-term convenerships and set periods of committee service. Many presbyteries, however, could do more to ring the changes among the directly appointed elders and use this form of recruitment to bring in individuals with particular gifts to serve for periods of two or three years. I also believe that we need to revisit the question of retired ministers retaining seats in presbytery. This is not to be ageist, but to make a point of principle. Retired teachers do not come back to the school for staff meetings. In the same way I fail to see on what basis ministers who have retired from the service of the Church should have a voice and a vote in determining the policy of the Church. Such a reform is, in my view, long overdue. This is not to say that retired ministers cannot continue to help out with locum work and pulpit supply, but the government of the Church is quite a different matter. Again, I make the point, that this is a criticism of the way the system operates at present. The good news is that within the system there are mechanisms for refreshment and renewal. In 1995 the Church came close to implementing this change, the proposal having received the support of a majority of presbyteries under the Barrier Act.[14] In the event, however, the General Assembly was persuaded, at the final hurdle, not to enact the necessary legislation.

In his *Practice and Procedure in the Church of Scotland* J. T. Cox lists three 'characteristic notes' of Presbyterianism.[15] The first of these is the principle of parity of ministers. Within the courts of the Church every ministerial member has equal right to speak and to vote. The moderator of the court presides over the business but does so as first among equals. In practice leaders emerge who, on the basis of experience or eloquence, carry authority and command respect, but even the Moderator of the General Assembly, traditionally regarded as the highest office in the Church, has no authority to instruct a minister in the exercise of his or her ministry. Only the relevant court can do that.

Another of Cox's characteristics takes this a stage further, and that is the equal participation in the higher courts of elders, and now deacons. I remember attending a General Assembly in the early years of my ministry, accompanied by a senior elder from my congregation. We voted differently in just about every division! I felt that his vote was cancelling out mine. No doubt he was thinking that my vote was cancelling out his! But that is the system, reflecting the doctrine of the priesthood of all believers with the ministry of word and sacrament exercised not over but within the life of the whole Church.

The third characteristic is the Church's conciliar polity and structure, with its hierarchy of courts, as distinct from a hierarchy of individuals. Sometimes, it has to be said, Presbyterians look wistfully, if not covetously, at a system which appears to give real responsibility and authority to individuals to make decisions. It is, perhaps, conceivable that a bishop will lie awake at night worrying about the state of the diocese. It is less likely that even the moderator of a presbytery will feel the same degree of 'ownership' of the presbytery. If a problem arises in a congregation the bishop can take control and impose a solution. The presbytery can do the same, but the mechanism invariably involves setting up the inevitable committee. However, this is somewhat simplistic. A number of friends who are bishops have expressed astonishment at Presbyterian notions of the practical authority they possess! By contrast, Presbyterian principles of parity and equal participation can have their own effectiveness.

While it is right and proper that we engage in a critical analysis of the operation of our Presbyterian polity I believe that there are positive strengths in what Cox describes as fundamental characteristics. One of the most telling speeches in the 2003 General Assembly debate on the Scottish Church Initiative for Union (SCIFU) was delivered by the Reverend Paraic Raemonn, a committed ecumenist and Director of Communication for the World Alliance of Reformed Churches. One might have expected Mr Raemonn to make a passionate speech in support of the scheme which envisioned a United Church of Scotland, embracing the Church of Scotland, the Scottish Episcopal Church, the United Reformed Church, the Methodist Church and the Churches of Christ. But that is not what we got. Rather, Mr Raemonn, while stressing his ecumenical credentials and commitment, suggested that SCIFU, with its goal of organic and structural unity, was based on a 1960s model of ecumenism. Today's thinking, he argued, was based much more on a model of churches working together. The General Assembly agreed and one outcome of this is that we are, perhaps, freer to affirm and to celebrate the positive and distinctive qualities of our Presbyterian heritage.

That said, a caveat must immediately be entered. All that we claim for Presbyterianism is that it is 'agreeable to the word of God'.[16] We do not claim that it is better than any other system of church government, still less that it is the only proper ecclesiastical polity. Any pride in the Presbyterian tradition is to be tempered by an appropriate Christian humility and an acceptance of the fact that we are but one tradition among many within the one, holy, catholic and apostolic Church.

It is, perhaps, not insignificant that Presbyterianism took root so readily in post-Reformation Scotland. Its principles of parity and participation sit well with a culture which has room for 'the lad o'pairts' and believes in its heart that 'a man's a man for a' that'. One of the most moving moments I recall in a General Assembly arose in 1985. It was during the course of a debate on abortion. Many men contributed to the discussion in speech and sermon. Then a woman rose. She was in the gallery to the Moderator's right. She began with the words: 'Moderator, I suspect I may be the only member of the Assembly who has actually had an abortion.' She spoke with great dignity and was listened to with great respect. A system which has room for such a voice in its highest court is a system of which we can be proud.

There is also respect for conscience and room for differing opinions. An important principle within the life of the Church is the recognition of liberty of opinion in matters which do not enter into the substance of the faith. For example, a position reached by the General Assembly on an issue such as abortion does not become binding on every member of the Church. At the height of the Section 28 controversy in 1999–2000 there were those who criticised the Church of Scotland for not speaking with one voice. But while some might view the tolerance of different voices as a weakness, others will argue that in such diversity is strength. The Presbyterian way is not to have an individual 'lay down the law' but to seek to discern the truth through prayer and deliberation guided by the Holy Spirit, at the same time having regard to right of conscience and liberty of opinion.

In this connection, though, it should be said that in those areas where the General Assembly has legislated, as distinct from taking a position on a matter of social or moral concern, the expectation is that all will abide by the law of the Church. This principle was clearly asserted in 1991, as already noted, in relation to the right of women to be considered for the eldership in exactly the same way as men. The conscience of some ministers in this matter was held not to overrule the entitlement of the women of the Church. Those who were unhappy were free to seek to change the law, but they were not free to deny women that which the Church as a whole, following due process, had granted to them.

THE FAITH OF THE CHURCH

What does the Church believe? I have devoted a later chapter of this book to this question, particularly as it has been raised in controversies over doctrinal standards such as the Westminster Confession of Faith. However, as this is a complex subject, it will be helpful, in this introductory chapter, to say a brief word on the matter.

The first thing to say is that the faith of the Church is expressed in life and action more than in words. On one occasion John the Baptist sent some of his disciples to ask Jesus whether he was the Messiah, or should they expect someone else. Jesus' answer wasn't a discourse on Old Testament teaching concerning a Messiah who was to come. Rather he told John's disciples to go back to their master and tell him what they had seen of Christ's healing ministry.[17] Of course, the faith of the Church is written down in creeds, confessions of faith and in the words of hymns and other devotional material, but, as has often been said, faith is caught rather than taught. Ultimately, faith is not a list of facts to be learned, but a way of life to be lived.

That way of life is discipleship of Jesus Christ. The world's three great monotheistic religions are Judaism, Christianity and Islam. All three trace their spiritual ancestry to Abraham. Judaism and Islam, while acknowledging one God, attach great honour and reverence to prophets and teachers such as Moses and Jesus. In the case of Islam the prophet Mohammed is also revered in this way. Where Christianity becomes distinctive is in its understanding of Jesus as more than a prophet, indeed, as God in human form, the Eternal Word made flesh. In the life of Christ, characterised by a generous grace and love reaching out to all, including those considered quite unlovable to many, Christian people have a model for their own living. It is a high ideal to which many fail to live up; yet the ideal remains both worthy and valid.

But faith is based not only on the life and example of Jesus Christ but also on the profound mystery of his death and resurrection. Christians believe that in the crucifixion we see God (for God is in Christ) entering fully into the sufferings of the world. Christians also believe that in the resurrection of Jesus Christ we find not simply an assurance of life beyond death but a promise that, ultimately, life and love will triumph over hatred and death. We believe further, that the power which was in Christ was poured out upon his followers at Pentecost[18] and that the Holy Spirit continues as a force for good in the life of the world. Putting all of this together, whereas Judaism and Islam hold that God is one, Christians believe that God is both Unity and Trinity. We believe that the 'Father God' of the Old Testament is also manifested as 'God the Son' in Jesus Christ and 'God the Holy Spirit', the light and guide of the Church in the world today. So, we worship one God who is Father, Son and Holy Spirit.

Like all churches the Church of Scotland gives a central place to the Bible. This library of sixty-six books, covering a period of around a thousand years in composition, contains different strands of writing, including history, wisdom literature, poetry and letters. It is known throughout the Church as the Word of God, and Christians certainly believe that God speaks through its writings. This is why readings from the Bible form part of every church service and why it is also an essential element in personal prayer and devotion. However, there is a difference of view among believers as to whether every word in the Bible *is* the literal Word of God, or whether that Word is, rather, *contained in* the

Bible. Those who hold to the former view are sometimes referred to as 'fundamentalists'. The official position of the Church of Scotland is that the Word is contained in the Bible, and when ministers are ordained one of the questions they are asked is: 'Do you believe the Word of God, which is contained in the Scriptures of the Old and New Testaments to be the supreme rule of faith and life?'

It is partly because of differing views of the Bible that Christians disagree on issues like the ordination of women, attitudes to homosexuality and inter-faith relations. Those who believe the Bible *is* the Word of God regard its statements as valid for all time coming, for example, in relation to women not speaking in Church[19] or, with regard to other religions, statements of Jesus like 'No one comes to the Father but by me.'[20] Those who take the 'contained in' view will study the context in which certain things were said, separating out material which they consider reflects the cultural values of the ancient world from the timeless truths of the Gospel. This, of course, is putting things very simply and, in reality, many Christians are in neither one camp nor the other but straddle both. For example the Archbishop of Canterbury, Dr Rowan Williams, has been described as theologically conservative but socially liberal, a description which would fit many people I know.

What is sad is when different groups within the Church appear to forget key Gospel words, such as 'love' and 'grace'. Jesus once urged his disciples that they should love one another that the world might believe.[21] The reality is that quarrels and disagreements among Christians, and religious people generally, have done much to turn people away from faith altogether. In our Church today, mercifully, disagreements do not lead to physical violence (as they did in the seventeenth century), but harsh and hurtful words are still spoken, with some claiming that they alone are truly Christian while others are undermining the Gospel. Since 1929 the reunited Church of Scotland has been a 'broad church', with room for diversity, liberty of opinion and a culture which enables differing theological perspectives to live and work together in common service of the Gospel. It is much to be hoped that this tradition can be maintained.

NOTES

1 G. D. Henderson, *The Claims of the Church of Scotland*, London: Hodder & Stoughton, 1951, p. 7. Reproduced by permission of Hodder & Stoughton.

2 Henderson, *Claims*, p. 2. Reproduced by permission of Hodder & Stoughton.

3 J. T. Cox, *Practice and Procedure in the Church of Scotland*, 6th edn, ed. D. F. M. MacDonald, Edinburgh: Church of Scotland, 1976, p. 1.

4 Henderson, *Claims*, p. 2.

5 A fuller account of these matters is given in the subsequent chapters on the General Assembly and Doctrine.

6 The oath required burgesses (citizens) of certain towns to acknowledge the true religion publicly preached within the realm and authorised by law. Some saw this as affirming the Established Church and refused to take the oath (anti-burghers), at the same time excommunicating those who did (burghers).

7 T. M. Devine, *The Scottish Nation 1700–2000*, London: Allen Lane, 1999, pp. 73, 90.

8 Robin Jenkins, *The Awakening of George Darroch*, Edinburgh: Waterfront in association with the Glasgow Herald, 1985.

9 Church of Scotland Act, 1921, section 2.

10 *The Second Book of Discipline*, 1578, VII, 40.

11 J. H. S. Burleigh, *A Church History of Scotland*, London: Oxford University Press, 1960, p. 178.

12 Report of Special Commission anent Review and Reform, Assembly Reports, 2001, p. 36/16, popularly known as *Church without Walls*.

13 Congregations, often old and historic charges, in which both matters spiritual and temporal are administered by the Kirk Session.

14 The Barrier Act dates from 1697 and requires that innovations in church law affecting worship, government, doctrine and discipline be referred to presbyteries. Only if a majority of presbyteries approve proposals agreed by the General Assembly can the next year's Assembly enact them into law, though it is not obliged to do so.

15 Cox, *Practice and Procedure*, p. 7.

16 See Chapter 10, Appendix 2: Preamble Questions and Formula used in Ordination and Induction Services (p. 185).

17 Matthew 11:4–6; Luke 7:18–23.

18 See Acts 2.

19 See 1 Corinthians 14:32–7.

20 John 14:6.

21 John 13:35.

2

A Church Reformed and Reforming

REFORMATA SEMPER REFORMANDA

One of the principles of a reformed church is the recognition that it is in continuing need of reform. Reformation is not something which happened at a moment in history, but an ongoing process. An old Latin phrase, *ecclesia reformata semper reformanda* (a church reformed, yet always in need of reform), gives classic expression to this notion. This rule has applied in the life of the Church of Scotland, as styles of worship and patterns of congregational life have developed over the centuries. The past thirty years have been particularly busy in this regard.

I was ordained to the ministry and inducted to my first charge of Menstrie, in the wee county of Clackmannanshire, on 2 June 1971. My own early efforts at reform were not promising. The interim moderator, the recently retired Reverend William Turner of Gargunnock, was to become a real 'father in God' to me over the next thirty years, but things did not get off to an auspicious start. He informed me that, as was customary in the case of a newly ordained minister, the congregation wished to present me with robes. I said I was delighted to accept and wondered if I might have a blue cassock, rather than the (then) traditional black. After a rather long pause the reply came: 'Macdonald, if you want to buy your own robes you can have canary yellow, but if the congregation is providing them you will have black!' That was me told.

My first attempt at organisational change was no more successful. At an early meeting of the Congregational Board I suggested that we should appoint some committees, including a finance committee. A canny farmer, Jimmy Gellatly by name, responded: 'Whit dae we need a Finance Committee for? We dinna hae ony finance!' In fairness, I should add that Jimmy was a committed and generous elder who, I discovered after his death, had quietly seen to it that the kirk books balanced at the end of each year.

Into the Seventies

As, in such modest ways, I was trying to introduce colour to worship and efficiency to congregational management, the Church of Scotland as a whole was engaging with a report which had been presented to the General Assembly of 1971 – the Anderson Report. This was the report of a Special Commission of twenty persons, set up by the Assembly of 1969, with the remit 'to examine priorities in mission in Scotland for the 'seventies and to make recommendations for action'. The Commission was chaired by Professor Hugh Anderson of New College and the official title given to the report was 'Keeping Pace with Tomorrow'. Another of my earliest ministerial memories is of a presbytery conference devoted to the study of the report, and a sense of excitement and anticipation that the Church was moving forward positively into the 1970s.

It is interesting to re-read the Anderson Report today and realise just how much the world has moved on. For example, there are echoes of old controversies, with comment on the World Council of Churches' funding of 'guerrilla movements', a reference to a special fund to combat racism, particularly in southern Africa. Nelson Mandela would have been one of those 'terrorists'. How quickly yesterday's 'guerrillas' become today's 'freedom fighters'!

Of more direct ecclesiastical interest, the report speaks bluntly of 'the current *malaise* of the Church'. The Church is described as 'a community of nostalgia' and there is a warning that, for increasing numbers of people 'caught up in the currents of change', the Church 'seems so rooted in the past that they cannot relate it to their present, far less to their future'. To address this predicament twenty-four recommendations were made. These called for the encouragement of team ministries, for more co-operation among local ministers and congregations, a greater affirmation of specialist chaplaincies, particularly in industry, and a review of the whole place of children in worship, the last mentioned combined with some rather negative comment on the traditional children's address. In addition the report identified four key areas of society with which the Church needed to engage seriously. These were industry, education, communications and mass media and, finally, politics. In words which seem even more relevant and urgent today the report opined:

> The great areas of life which have become virtually closed to the Church (industry, the young generation, urban masses) must be appreciated for what they are and on their own terms, not just as providing potential church members. Integral to the dynamics of mission is as fully professional an understanding as the Church can muster of the concrete circumstances in which it is placed. Mission initiatives will be frustrated if we ignore the increased understanding of the world afforded by sociology, psychology, educational theory and communications, and the impact of technology on contemporary human relationships.[1]

The Committee of Forty

The same General Assembly which received the Anderson Report in 1971 also received a report from the Church and Nation Committee which successfully proposed

> that a special commission, widely representative of all sections of Church life, including younger ministers and elders, be set up to interpret for the Church the purpose towards which God is calling his people in Scotland, to investigate and assess the resources of the Church in persons and in property and to make recommendations for the reshaping of the life and structure of the Church, and so to enable her to make her testimony to the Gospel more effective in the life of the changing world.[2]

The Anderson Commission had twenty members. This new Commission was given forty members and thus became known as the Committee of Forty. Its convener was another theologian, Professor Robin Barbour of the Chair of New Testament at Aberdeen.

The Committee of Forty delivered six comprehensive and challenging reports to the General Assemblies of 1973 to 1978 and, in many ways, set the agenda and the shape of the Church for the next twenty years. There was in its core task of 'discerning God's purpose in a changed and changing situation' an echo of an earlier Commission, 'For the Interpretation of God's Will in the Present Crisis', set up during the Second World War and convened by Professor John Baillie. Certainly, the sense of *kairos* (critical time) is very strong throughout the various reports, set as they are against a background of the cold war, nuclear weapons, sexual liberation, violence, increasing affluence and diminishing religious commitment, as well as issues surrounding Scotland's political aspirations and direction. Reflecting on the Church's declining influence the report observes with a shrewd hopefulness, 'Where the Church cannot dominate, the truth she guards can be seen anew'.[3] The Committee also acknowledged, in a way Anderson did not, the importance of the ecumenical dimension and warns, again in a sharp phrase, 'our self-sufficiency could be the death of us'. Rather,

> to go out on mission is not to draw people into existing institutions (though that will be one part of it so long as present institutions exist); it is to go out in search of a fullness of life which we have not yet found, which God has in store for us.[4]

That said, both Anderson and the Committee of Forty could not and did not ignore institutional and organisational questions. Anderson is wary of any notion

> that more efficient organisation or more streamlined administration will guarantee the advance of God's purpose for the liberation of men [sic] as we find it in Christ. Still, we are committed to ask, whether present structures do not frustrate our task of reaching men and, if so, whether they have not become idols.[5]

The Committee of Forty declared:

> Our study of the central structures has been founded on the assumption that the primary objective of change must be the renewal of the place of mission throughout the whole Church. Consequently, economy in money and manpower must be seen as a means of freeing resources and not as an end in itself.[6]

The Committee went on to identify 'the key to renewal . . . in the re-establishment of the presbytery as the focus of mission' and concluded that 'this in turn requires a radical revision of the central structure which tends to draw power to itself'.[7]

In 1975, three years before the presentation of the Committee of Forty's final report, presbyteries had been reorganised so as to follow the new pattern of local government introduced into Scotland at the time. The aim of the reorganisation was to ensure that the structure of the Church related as closely as possible to the structure of civil society. Thus presbyteries were reconfigured to reflect district council boundaries while synods related to the larger regional authorities. These changes were not specifically proposals of the Committee, but clearly what we now call 'joined-up thinking' was occurring. Presbytery reorganisation had been mentioned in Anderson and was also quite specifically raised by way of an Overture in the General Assembly of 1971.

While the Committee of Forty's intention was to modify the central committee structure of the Church, with a view to enabling a transfer of power to presbyteries, it is arguable that, in reality, what happened was precisely the opposite. Certainly there was no denying the need to rationalise a system of forty-seven separate committees all reporting to the General Assembly and consuming 9,000 'man-hours [sic] of meetings'. These needed to be converted 'into a more economic and effective structure'.[8] The body entrusted with this task was to be a new Assembly Council, charged 'to enable the General Assembly to be more effective in directing, supporting and encouraging the whole Church in its work of service and mission'. More specifically, this 'slim, sleek, svelte' Council (as it was memorably described by a prominent convener, hostile to its creation) was to organise the multiplicity of committees into a small number of operating and servicing boards, and thereafter to keep their effectiveness under review. The conveners of the new boards would sit on the Council along with members who were to be directly elected by the General Assembly, and the Secretary of the Council would be 'the chief executive at the Church offices'.[9] With some modification the new structure of boards and committees came into being in 1980 and continues, largely unchanged, to the present, when it is again under review.

As noted above, far from releasing power to presbyteries as the Committee of Forty had hoped, the creation of what have recently been described as 'fortress boards' became, effectively, quite disempowering of the local church, leading to the critique contained in *Church without Walls*, with its reminder that the centre is there to serve the local church, and not the other way around.

> The current model, [that report argues] assumes a top down pattern of governance – from centre to presbytery to local congregation. We recommend that the shape of the church be turned upside down to affirm the primacy of the local Christian community, supported appropriately by Presbytery and central administration.[10]

Church without Walls, rightly, challenged a paralysing culture which resulted in congregations feeling that they required permission from 'higher up' before developing local initiatives or, indeed, feeling that their role was simply to respond to initiatives from the centre. The Committee of Forty's concern over 9,000 person-hours spent on attendance at committee meetings, not to mention sub-committees and working groups, has also not been seriously addressed. At the turn of the millennium, two Assembly Boards (Ministry and Social Responsibility) had over ninety members. This reflects, yet again, the Presbyterian disease of 'institutionalised distrust' with every presbytery having a representative and Assembly-appointed members over and above. It remains highly questionable as to whether this is a good use of people's time and makes for effective decision-making.

The new Assembly Council also came up against suspicion and resistance as it sought to engage with its remit. It was not long before the direct election of members by the Assembly was abandoned in favour of the traditional (safer?) process of appointment through the Nomination Committee. Inevitably boards did not welcome having their operations subject to regular review and conveners found themselves caught 'between a rock and a hard place' when, having agreed to something in the Council, they subsequently discovered that their own boards were not happy at what they perceived to be a threat to their own interests. Matters came to a head in the General Assembly of 1995 when carefully balanced budget proposals, agreed by the Council after much soul-searching and painful negotiation, were lost on the floor of the General Assembly following a rebellion by those bodies most affected. At the same time, the impending retirement of the then Principal Clerk had precipitated a decision to set up a Special Commission to review the Assembly Council itself, the Board of Practice and Procedure and the relationship between them.

The Simpson Commission

This Commission, convened by the Very Reverend Dr James Simpson, reported to the General Assembly of 1996. The conclusion of its review of the Assembly Council was that it had become overly immersed in the management of the Church's central organisation and, as a consequence, had lost sight of the Committee of Forty's original vision for it, as a body charged 'to enable the General Assembly to be more effective in directing, supporting and encouraging the whole Church in its work of service and mission'. The Commission therefore proposed, and the Assembly agreed, that the Council should be relieved of the management elements of its remit and should be reconstituted as a 'think-tank' for the Church. Accordingly, its new remit was 'to assess the changing needs, challenges and responsibilities of the Church, to identify priority areas and tasks and to make recommendations to the General Assembly', and to do so in consultation with bodies such as presbyteries, congregations, boards and other denominations. The Commission also recommended the creation of a new body, to be called the Co-ordinating Forum, the membership of which would comprise the conveners and secretaries of all the Assembly boards and committees. The Forum was to meet at least twice in the year, with one meeting being residential. The Council would consult with the Forum in its work of identifying the priorities of the Church. The Board of Stewardship and Finance was also to seek the views of the Forum as it prepared the Church's budget for ensuing years. Over and above these formal functions the Forum would provide a mechanism whereby those charged with responsibility for different aspects of the Church's work at national level could get to know one another, share information and so enable a more coordinated approach to their work. In this way it was hoped that a culture, once described as 'co-operative autonomy', might be transcended.

The new-style Assembly Council approached its work on a consultative basis at various levels and this is reflected in its reports to the

General Assembly from 1997 onwards. Through the Co-ordinating Forum the Council has also led the Church to a point where priorities have been agreed, the key priority being 'to ensure that the Gospel story continues to be told and lived out in Scotland' and to do this 'by nurturing worshipping and witnessing communities'.[11] Significantly, the Council has achieved a new approach to budgeting by establishing the principle that funding will follow areas of work, rather than simply maintaining the existing board and committee structure. Areas of work have been identified, such as parish staffing, congregational resourcing, church and society, support services, social work, ecumenical and overseas work and, at time of writing, the Council is engaged in discussions as to how best to reshape the board and committee structure to facilitate this work efficiently, effectively, economically and in ways which truly demonstrate that it is the function of the centre to support the local and not the other way around.

The removal of the Council's management responsibilities in 1996 left a gap which concerned many. Who now would exercise control over such matters as staff appointments at '121'? Who would review the work of the various boards and committees? It is perhaps significant that between 1996 and 2001 no less than three General Assembly Commissions were set up, in response to petitions, to investigate the workings of different boards. As a result, thought is, yet again, being given to the creation of some kind of Assembly executive body, to which real decision-making responsibilities could be delegated between General Assemblies. These responsibilities could include approving new staff appointments in the church offices and determining the budget of the Church. Such a body might also be given a remit to keep the whole operation of the central administration under review.

As implied, the idea is by no means new. In the past the Church has commissioned economic surveys and reports from management consultants and business-oriented ideas have been brought forward, including a proposal to introduce 'a chief executive' to the central administration. Most recently, a Special Commission on the Board of Communication, reporting to the General Assembly of 1999, urged that further thought be given to such an appointment, but the

Assembly declined even to consider the matter. This whole episode is both interesting and instructive. In 1996 the membership of the Board of Communication had been reduced from forty-two to twelve with a requirement that 'such members [should] have knowledge of, or expertise, or particular interest, in the work of communication and its management, with particular reference to commercial activities'.[12] The new, streamlined Board set about its business with a commercial will and soon came across resistance, leading to a staff petition to the General Assembly of 1998. (This resulted in the Special Commission referred to above.) The same year the Board itself recommended an increase in its membership from twelve to eighteen. It recalled the decision to reduce from forty-two to twelve based on 'the need to make relatively speedy decisions on matters which often have a commercial dimension', but now observed that 'recent events have raised concerns that the distinctive elements of the Church's representational approach have been lost to some extent'.[13] This offers a good illustration of a comment in the *Church without Walls* report of 2001: 'the Church is operating with two cultures: the Presbyterian ethos that resists personal leadership, and a business organisation at the heart of its administration which requires executive powers'.[14]

Yet again, we come back to the description of Presbyterianism as 'institutionalised distrust' and 'the government of the few by the many'. Under current arrangements the chief executive of the Church is the General Assembly itself, and many believe, as the Committee of Forty itself pointed out in the 1970s, that the centres of power within the organisation are difficult to identify and, consequently, not readily accountable. It has been said that to be answerable only to the General Assembly is not to be answerable at all. I am not convinced of that, having seen conveners given some rough rides when the Assembly thought it was not being given the whole story. At the same time I recognise that a constantly changing body of some 800 people which meets once a year, and whose decisions can be affected by emotional speeches, special pleading and the timing of a vote, is perhaps not the best mechanism for managing a multi-million pound organisation.

The General Assembly of 2003 gave a warm reception to the reforming proposals of the Assembly Council, and encouraged the Council and the Co-ordinating Forum to continue along the road upon which they had embarked and 'to formulate proposals for strategic planning, including the determination of priorities and structural change, and report to the General Assembly of 2004'.[15] The Assembly also accepted an addendum from a commissioner on the report of the Board of Stewardship and Finance. This gave 'powers to the Board to ensure, by such management action as it deems necessary, that the necessary budget cuts are effected by 2008'.[16] Time will tell whether successor General Assemblies continue the momentum towards a leaner central administration and manage to find a way of delegating some serious powers to an executive body (sleek, slim and svelte!) while continuing to function credibly as the Church's supreme court.

Auxiliary Ministry

One practical legacy of the Committee of Forty was the rationalising of the multi-committee structure of the General Assembly into the present-day boards. The other enduring legacy was the Auxiliary Ministry. The proposal was set out in the report to the 1977 General Assembly and the Committee was instructed to bring forward enabling legislation the following year. It was argued that part-time, non-stipendiary ministers

> could be of great assistance to the Church in meeting the needs of coming decades, not only for financial reasons but also, and more importantly, because new types of ministry could thereby be developed in urban as well as rural areas.[17]

It was stressed that the ministry envisaged 'must not be a second-rate affair' and also that 'no pool of willing but unused candidates must be created'. Rather the new ministry 'would operate only in situations where it was seen to be needed by the relevant Kirk Session(s) and Presbytery, and where suitable candidates were available'.[18]

The scheme was implemented in 1980, very much along the lines proposed, and over the years has enabled the deployment of many gifted people within the Church's ministry of word and sacrament.

However, there have also been tales of difficulty, disappointment and frustration, as support for the scheme has varied from presbytery to presbytery. From time to time questions have arisen as to what precisely is meant by 'non-stipendiary'. For example, can an auxiliary minister be deployed in a chaplaincy post paid for outwith the Church? Questions of status have arisen in between appointments. May an auxiliary minister, not currently in an appointment, officiate at a wedding by private invitation? A need for some rationalising of the Church's various ministries has also been acknowledged – readers, deacons, elders who are authorised by their presbyteries to conduct worship. How do these offices and functions relate to each other and to the auxiliary ministry?

In 2003 the Board of Ministry presented a review of the Auxiliary Ministry to the General Assembly. In this review the Board affirmed 'the importance of the Auxiliary Ministry' as a ministry alongside and in partnership with the full-time ministry and the diaconate and addressed issues which required clarification. It was recognised, for example, that an Auxiliary Minister could serve as a locum or interim moderator, that a retired Auxiliary Minister could retain his or her seat in presbytery and that modest honoraria could be paid. Procedures for transferring from the auxiliary to the whole-time ministry were also introduced.

Church without Walls

The General Assembly of 1999 met in the Edinburgh International Conference Centre (EICC). This was in order to allow the newly elected Scottish Parliament to remain in the Assembly Hall which had become its temporary home. Some complained that the seating in the EICC was too comfortable! The venue, with its state-of-the-art conference facilities, certainly offered a very different ambience from the Assembly Hall. Perhaps it was entirely coincidental, but this General Assembly, meeting in this very modern place, decided to support a forward-looking proposal from the Presbytery of Edinburgh that a special commission be established to re-examine in depth the primary purposes of the Church and the shape of the Church of Scotland as we enter into the next millennium; to formulate proposals for a process of continuing reform; to consult on such matters with other Scottish Churches; and to report to the General Assembly of 2001.

Prior to the Assembly there had been some discussion as to whether the work envisaged for the proposed commission was, in effect, the same work which was already being undertaken by the Assembly Council. The general consensus was that this was indeed the case (it was also the view of the Assembly Council!), with the result that what was put to the Assembly was the appointment of the new Commission and the discharge of the Council. However, the Assembly knows best and, in its wisdom, decided that there was room for both bodies. In the event, that has turned out to be a wise decision. The Commission, knowing that it had two years of life, approached its task with urgency, energy and enthusiasm. Sensibly both the Commission and the Council appointed observers to each other's meetings and, once the Commission had finished its work, the Council became the effective guardian of its legacy. The Reverend Peter Neilson was appointed to convene the Special Commission anent Review and Reform (to give it its full title) and, as already noted, the report which appeared two years later was given the popular title *Church without Walls*.

Church without Walls did not so much produce proposals for concrete change, as seek to stimulate new ways of thinking about the life of the Church. It sought to 'return the ministry of the Church to the people of God . . . to give them the tools and the trust to shape a vision for the church in their own area'. The best way to achieve this, the report maintained was 'by allowing congregations the space and opportunity to develop their own patterns of ministry, mission, worship and leadership that best suits the people and situations where they are'.[19]

This emphasis on the local church goes to the heart of the report. This is 'the focus of action', with the regional church as the focus of support and the central church as the focus of servicing. The primary calling of the Church was to follow Christ and church members should see themselves not so much as members of an institution but as disciples of Jesus Christ in the world. There was a need for flexibility in structure and organisation, but, the Commission warned, little would be achieved by changes in the structures unless mindsets also changed. There are distinct echoes here of the Committee of Forty. In mindset-changing spirit, the report was made available in work-book format as a basis for reflection and discussion in church groups around the country.

Like the Committee of Forty the Commission also left a practical legacy in the shape of the Parish Development Fund. This fund, set up in 2003, with £1 million and with an additional £0.5 million going in annually over the subsequent four years, will give grants to fund local mission projects initiated by congregations. It is a tangible commitment to the policy of trusting and encouraging the local church.

'Tomorrow's Presbyteries'

The final reforming initiative to mention in this chapter is the report entitled, 'Tomorrow's Presbyteries', presented to the General Assembly of 2001. The genesis of this lay in a remit given to the Board of Practice and Procedure to undertake a fresh examination of presbytery boundaries. As already noted, these had last been revised in 1975, in light of the new local government organisation which took effect that year. Local government boundaries had now been further revised. Furthermore, concerns were being expressed by some smaller presbyteries that they were barely viable and faced real difficulties in matters such as provision of interim moderators.

The Board reported the following year and sought an extension of the remit to include a review of the role and function of presbyteries, and to do so on an inter-board basis with Ministry, National Mission and Parish Education. The outcome was a radical report which argued for fewer (perhaps as few as seven) presbyteries, but with the much larger presbyteries being given responsibility for managing regional budgets. Thus, for example, each presbytery would have its ministry aid budget and decisions as to the allocation of aid within the region would be made entirely by the presbytery. The group argued that such larger presbyteries would require regional support in terms of professional services and administration, but that there should be a corresponding reduction in the size of the central administration in Edinburgh.

On various grounds the proposals did not find favour but a series of well-attended 'road shows' around the country in the autumn of 2001 did stimulate much lively discussion. This, combined with *Church without Walls* and the ongoing consultation programme of the Assembly Council, helped to foster a changing mindset which saw change not as something inevitable to be resisted until the last possible moment but as something to be embraced as being of the essence of a church which is truly reformed and reforming. In the event a gradual realignment of presbyteries is taking place in response to local circumstances. In June 2003 the Presbyteries of Greenock and Paisley united and in early 2004 the presbyteries of South Argyll, Dunoon, and Lorn and Mull came together to form the Presbytery of Argyll. At the time of writing, other mergers are under consideration.

NOTES

1 Assembly Reports, 1971, p. 697.
2 Assembly Reports, 1971, p. 172.
3 Assembly Reports, 1978, p. 495.
4 Assembly Reports, 1978, p. 501.
5 Assembly Reports, 1971, p. 680.
6 Assembly Reports, 1978, p. 505.
7 Assembly Reports, 1978, p. 505.
8 Assembly Reports, 1978, p. 506.
9 Assembly Reports, 1978, p. 507.
10 Assembly Reports, 2001, p. 36/16.
11 Assembly Reports, 2003, p. 11/4.
12 General Assembly Standing Orders of the time.
13 Assembly Reports, 1998, p. 26/5.
14 Assembly Reports, 2001, p. 36/36.
15 Deliverance of General Assembly 2003 on Report of the Assembly Council.
16 Deliverance of General Assembly 2003 on Report of Board of Stewardship and Finance.
17 Assembly Reports, 1978, p. 513.
18 Assembly Reports, 1978, p. 513.
19 Assembly Reports, 2001, p. 36/8.

3

The Kirk's Global Reach

LOCAL AND GLOBAL

In the General Assembly of 1995 a significant exchange took place during the debate on the report of the Assembly Council. That year the Council came forward with a series of proposals for a major redistribution of the funding allocated to various areas of work. An additional £400,000 was to be given to the Aid budget of the Committee on the Maintenance of the Ministry, the fund which paid ministers of congregations unable to meet the full stipend costs themselves. The bulk of this money was to be found by making cuts, totalling £350,000, to the budgets of the boards of Communication, National Mission and World Mission. This reallocation was based on a prioritising of the Church's work by the previous year's General Assembly which had affirmed 'the church's primary task for the immediate future as mission to the people of Scotland'.[1] The Council now spelled this out even more bluntly by declaring its 'belief that the Church of Scotland has a primary responsibility to the people of Scotland in Scotland'.[2] From this premise the Council argued that priority must be given to ensuring an adequate supply of ordained ministers, lay field staff and necessary buildings. In presenting the report the Council Convener, the Reverend David Munro, underlined the point, by reminding the Assembly of the commitment contained in the third Declaratory Article, that the Church would 'bring the ordinances of religion to the people in every parish of Scotland through a territorial ministry'.

The Principal Clerk of the General Assembly, the Very Reverend Dr James Weatherhead, took issue with this argument, and pointed to the first of the Declaratory Articles, which, he maintained, logically took priority over the third. This first article proclaimed the Church of Scotland's place as 'part of the Holy Catholic or Universal Church' and then went on to enumerate various 'core functions' of the Church. These included the task of 'labouring for the advancement of the Kingdom of God throughout the world'. How, Dr Weatherhead wondered, did this declaration square with the Council's proposals to reduce the budget of the Board of World Mission by the sum of £140,000? And, with regard to the notion that the Church had a primary responsibility to the people of Scotland in Scotland Dr Weatherhead argued that the Church had never taken the view that charity begins at home. The outcome of the subsequent debate was the rejection of the Council's proposals.

Similar issues arose in the General Assembly of 2003. Through a process of reflection and consultation the (new-style)[3] Assembly Council had identified the Church's key priority as 'to ensure that the Gospel story continues to be told and lived out in Scotland by nurturing worshipping and witnessing communities'. From this the Council argued that a budget priority be given to ensuring adequate staffing and resourcing of parishes around Scotland, and the Assembly agreed with this view. However, echoes of the 1995 debate were clearly to be heard in deliverance, considered and approved later in the week, on the report of the Board of World Mission. This instructed that Board

> to enter into discussion with the Assembly Council, the Board of Stewardship and Finance and the Co-ordinating Forum on ways in which, at a time of emphasis on congregational resourcing and parish staffing, due consideration can be given to the expression of meaningful solidarity with partner churches in needy and strife-torn countries.

Clearly in putting forward this deliverance the Board of World Mission was putting down the same 'marker' as Dr Weatherhead eight years previously, namely, that a prioritising of ministry and mission within Scotland must not lead to a neglect, still less an abandonment, of the Church of Scotland's global vision and commitment.

THE KIRK IN ALL THE WORLD

The Church of Scotland has always had an international perspective. In the first chapter of this book we noted that Christianity came to Scotland in the late fourth century through the missionary work of Ninian. He established a church, known as *candida casa* (meaning 'the white house'), at Whithorn on the Solway. Very little is known about Ninian himself, but it is generally accepted that he studied in Rome, and the dedication of his church to St Martin suggests a knowledge of Martin of Tours. Perhaps he even visited Tours as he travelled through Gaul, on his return to Britain from Rome. That other great early saint of the Scottish church, Columba, came from Ireland, and the international dimension is also present in the patronal association of St Andrew with Scotland. Tradition tells of an eighth-century monk called Regulus or Rule, setting sail from Greece with some of the apostle's relics, and eventually arriving at Kilrymont (now St Andrews) on the east coast of Fife. By the time we come to the Middle Ages we can note that the saintly Queen Margaret was born in Hungary, the daughter of a Bavarian princess. By then (the late eleventh century) the Church of Scotland was part of the western Catholic Church administered from Rome, though during the notorious papal schism (1378–1417), when there were rival popes in Rome and Avignon, the Scottish Church's loyalty was to Avignon. This loyalty was rewarded when the Avignon Pope, Benedict XIII, granted the papal bull which established Scotland's first university. In his *History of the Church of Scotland to the Reformation*, John Duke depicts a colourful scene when he records:

> In 1413, amid scenes of unexampled rejoicing in St. Andrews, in which clergy and people joined – the singing of the *Te Deum* and the celebration of high mass, the lighting of bonfires and the ringing of bells – the bull arrived from Pope Benedict, which set the Papal seal upon the foundation of the first University of Scotland.[4]

In the Reformation period, too, there was a considerable coming and going between Scotland and mainland Europe, much of it in the form of forced exile, but it did mean that the first leaders of the reformed church were men with an international outlook. John Knox ministered in Frankfurt and Geneva. Andrew Melville taught in Geneva, and Patrick Hamilton studied in Paris before taking up a teaching appointment at St Andrews in 1523. George Wishart, on being accused of heresy, fled Montrose where he was teaching, making his way to Bristol, thence to Strasbourg, Basel, Zurich and Cambridge where he was a tutor at Corpus Christi College,[5] returning to Scotland and, like Patrick Hamilton, to martyrdom.

While contacts continued there was less international emphasis in the decades following the Reformation which, as we have seen, was a time of painful struggle between the different factions within the Church. James Bulloch and Andrew Drummond in *The Scottish Church 1688–1843* describe 'the century of the Covenant' (the seventeenth) as one in which 'Scots [were] isolated from foreign parts and absorbed in fighting each other'.[6] However, they also go on to note that ministers were included in the ill-fated Darien enterprise of 1698 and were expected not only to minister to their fellow Scots but also to extend their work to the natives of that part of central America. However, it was not really until the last decade of the eighteenth century and the early years of the nineteenth that the cause of foreign missions was taken up in a major way. Bodies such as the Baptist Missionary Society, the London Missionary Society, the Church Missionary Society and the British and Foreign Bible Society came into being during this period. Voices within the Church of Scotland, as well as the Relief and Secession Churches, were also raised in support of foreign missions. In 1829 the Church of Scotland's first missionary, Alexander Duff, was ordained for service in India, arriving in Calcutta in May 1830. In the ensuing decades Scottish missionaries travelled to what would have been regarded as the uttermost parts of the earth, in order to take the gospel to 'the heathen'. In the process they became national heroes, with names such as Alexander Duff, Robert Moffat, Robert Laws, David Livingstone and Mary Slessor becoming household words. Indeed, their fame continues to the present day.

If evangelical zeal was one factor in the developing global reach of the Scottish Church, the other was emigration, voluntary and involuntary. The notorious Highland clearances resulted in thousands of Scots being forcefully expelled from their native country and carried across the seas to places such as North America, Australia and New Zealand. Many Scots also found themselves transported to antipodean penal colonies, often for the pettiest of crimes. The record of the first residents of Fremantle Prison in Western Australia, a prison built by the transported convicts for their own occupancy, contains numerous entries such as 'John Macleod, semi-literate crofter, Isle of Lewis'. Others left Scotland of their own accord, to seek fame and fortune. Professor T. M. Devine notes that the early 1850s' gold rush attracted around 90,000 Scots to Australia.[7] Others went abroad as civil servants, diplomats, colonial officials and entrepreneurs, and it was natural that this diaspora should take its native culture with it. Presbyterian churches grew up, outposts of the mother church, and frequently replicating the differences and divisions back home. Not only in Scotland were the effects of the Disruption felt but throughout the world, wherever Presbyterian Scots had settled. The tradition of 'Scots Kirks' still lives on in many parts of the world. The majority of such churches, for example, St Andrew's, Nairobi, and the Scots Church in Melbourne, are now firmly incorporated within indigenous Presbyterian Churches. Others, such as St Andrew's, Colombo, and Greyfriars St Ann's, Port of Spain, remain as congregations of the Church of Scotland.

A perusal of the *Church of Scotland Year-Book* for 1900 lists Indian Mission Stations in Calcutta, Darjeeling, Kalimpong, Madras, Panjab [sic], Sialkot, Daska, Gujarat, Chamba and Poona, together with Missions in East Africa, British Central Africa and China. There are also reports of Jewish Mission work in Constantinople, Smyrna, Salonica, Beirut and Alexandria. There is even listed a Jewish Mission in 'Glasgow and its Neighbourhood'. The 1950 *Year-Book* contains a formidable list (eleven pages) of missionaries serving overseas, but also provides details of the presbyteries of Northern Europe, Southern Europe, Spain and Portugal, Bengal, Eastern Himalaya, Rajputana, Punjab and North-West Frontier province, Western India, Madras, the Gold Coast, Calabar, South Africa, Livingstonia, Kenya Colony, Manchuria, Jamaica, Jerusalem, Blantyre (Nyasaland)

and South America. This impressive global reach certainly says something about the Church of Scotland at the midpoint of the twentieth century.

Over the years since then, as already noted, the Church has gradually encouraged congregations around the world, whether established by Scottish missionaries or Scottish emigrants, to become part of the local Presbyterian Church. Indeed, it would be true to say, in many cases, that the indigenous Presbyterian Church grew out of the Church of Scotland mission and presbytery. Such churches have continued to grow prodigiously and, in numerical terms, churches such as the Church of Central Africa Presbyterian, the Presbyterian Church of East Africa, the Presbyterian Church of Korea and the Presbyterian Church (USA) are now much larger than the Church of Scotland. In addition, movements with Church of Scotland roots find expression in such significant churches as the Church of South India, the Church of North India, the United Church of Canada, the Presbyterian Church in Canada, the Uniting Church of Australia, the Presbyterian Church of Australia and the United Church of Zambia. Extraordinary dynamism is to be found in such churches as the Presbyterian Church of Nigeria, the Presbyterian Church of Singapore and the Presbyterian Church of Ghana, through whose witness many new congregations are being formed and new areas reached in Christian witness. Being part of such an extensive and dynamic movement of faith is surely something which can give the Kirk confidence as it grapples with fresh missionary challenges closer to home.

While there is, therefore, no Church of Scotland presence as such in North and South America, in Africa, India, Pakistan, Australia or New Zealand the legacy is apparent and the links are strong. A small number of Church of Scotland congregations do remain, however, in Colombo (Sri Lanka), Port of Spain (Trinidad and Tobago), Bermuda and the Bahamas. Being too isolated from each other to be grouped sensibly into a presbytery, these are overseen by the Board of World Mission direct. In addition, two overseas presbyteries remain, namely, Europe and Jerusalem. The viability of these was examined by the Board of Practice and Procedure between 2000 and 2003 and the

General Assembly accepted the Board's recommendation that they should continue. In the case of the European charges there was felt to be sufficient contiguity and cohesion to support a valid presbyterial relationship, and therefore no need for each charge to be overseen by the Board of World Mission direct. In the case of Jerusalem, which has only two charges in Jerusalem and Tiberias, it was recognised that any perceived downgrading of the status of the Church of Scotland's presence in Israel could have negative implications for broader Christian witness in the region.

Following a decision of the General Assembly of 1999 a major development programme has been undertaken on the church and hospice at Tiberias with a view to meeting the requirements of contemporary pilgrims, showing solidarity with the local Christian community and providing a much needed place of cross-cultural encounter and reconciliation. While the *intifada*, which began in 2000, has largely kept pilgrims away, the Board of World Mission's hope is that this will prove a sound investment for the future. St Andrew's, Jerusalem, was dedicated, on St Andrew's Day 1930, as a memorial to 'the men and women of Scottish blood who gave their lives for the deliverance of the Holy Land',[8] and was paid for by public subscription. It is a popular venue for pilgrims in 'normal' times, and provides a highly valued ministry across the Palestinian/Israeli divide. The various Scots Kirks around mainland Europe continue to meet expatriate, indigenous and international needs, providing English-language reformed worship in prominent European cities. Many of these congregations have entered into formal partnership agreements with local churches. For the record, the congregations within the Presbytery of Europe are to be found in Amsterdam, Brussels, Budapest, Fuengirola (Costa del Sol), Geneva, Gibraltar, Lausanne, Lisbon, Malta, Paris, Rome, Rotterdam and Turin. For sake of completeness, when referring to the Church's presence beyond Scotland, it should also be noted that there is a Presbytery of England with charges in Corby, Guernsey, Jersey, Liverpool, London and Newcastle upon Tyne. The congregations in Berwick-upon-Tweed and Carlisle are within the presbyteries of Duns and Annandale and Eskdale respectively.

PARTNERSHIP

A key word in defining international connections today is 'partnership'. The word is used to characterise the relationship between the Church of Scotland and other churches around the world. While it may be fair, both historically and emotionally, to describe the Church of Scotland as 'the mother church of Presbyterianism', the reality is that the Kirk stands in a relationship of equality and mutual respect with other Presbyterian (and non-Presbyterian) churches around the world. In 1999 the Church of Scotland hosted a significant partner churches conference in St Andrews, and this enabled the Board of World Mission to identify a number of priority areas for partnership in mission. These related to theological education, evangelism, holistic mission (that is, enabling one another to respond with Christian compassion to human needs in our rapidly changing societies), mission in pluralistic societies (that is, strengthening Christian identity in our multi-religious and multi-cultural societies by supporting one another and sharing our experiences), prophetic ministry and the sharing of human and material resources. At the same time the Board listed its strategic commitments for the decade, 2001–10, as follows:

- Working with partner churches on new initiatives in evangelism
- Working for justice, peace and reconciliation in situations of conflict or threat
- Resourcing the Church to set people free from the oppression of poverty
- Contributing meaningfully to the struggle against the HIV/AIDS epidemic
- Increasing the involvement of Scottish Christians in the world Church[9]

It is also relevant to quote from the Board's Statement of Identity and Purpose:

There are many ways in which partnership in mission can be expressed, but the Board places a priority on 'saying it with people'. Many partner churches have affirmed this policy and pointed out that, without the warmth of human relationships, a partner relationship soon grows cold and loses dynamism. Partner churches continue to make requests for mission partners to come from Scotland to fill strategic posts in their outreach.

It should be noted that the phrase 'mission partner' is used nowadays in preference to the term 'missionary'. The focus is no longer on a unilateral mission to 'heathen lands', but on a two-way flow of people, ideas and resources as partner churches seek to strengthen each other in witness to Jesus Christ. The 2003–2004 *Church of Scotland Year Book* lists ministers, church development workers, doctors, teachers, nurses, administrators and others, sent out and supported by the Church of Scotland, and working with churches in Africa, Asia, the Caribbean, Central and South America and the Middle East. The list is not so long as the one already referred to in the 1950 *Year Book*, filling five, rather than eleven pages, but it is impressive nonetheless. In this connection it is also relevant to mention Scottish Churches World Exchange, an ecumenical endeavour through which, over the past twenty years, more than a thousand (mostly young) people from Scotland have served on a voluntary basis, usually for a year, with an overseas partner church. While this is, as already noted, an ecumenical body, it is fair to say that it has been mainly staffed and funded from the Church of Scotland and the majority of volunteers have been Church of Scotland members.

In its report to the General Assembly of 2003 the Board of World Mission reflected at a very practical level on the meaning of partnership in a world such as ours, and stated its conviction: 'In a human community, more than ever aware of its global interdependence, there is an opportunity to make known the meaning of the gospel by demonstrating the kind of partnership which faith in Jesus Christ makes possible.' The report continued: 'Knowing that many of our partner churches are facing serious issues of conflict within their societies at this time, the Board has been challenged as to how to be a good partner to churches witnessing in conflict situations.'[10] Partnership, of course, works two ways and recent initiatives such as the 'Faithshare' programme have provided opportunities for people to come from overseas and serve with congregations in Scotland, an experience which many will acknowledge to be mutually enriching. The fact is that, today, Christianity in Africa and Asia, mission fields in the nineteenth century, reflects a dynamism and energy which is less evident in the mainline churches of twenty-first century Europe.

Reference should also be made to the Scottish Churches' China Group (SCCG) – a significant and exciting development over the past thirty years. Thirty years ago all links between the Church of Scotland and China had been broken by the Communist Revolution. However, over the past twenty years, as China has reopened to the outside world, there have been opportunities for sensitive involvement. Notably through the Amity Foundation, a steady stream of Scots has served for periods of time in China, usually in the medical and educational fields. At the same time, the SCCG has hosted Chinese healthcare professionals and others who have come for study and training in Scotland. These ties of friendship and co-operation provide a basis in which the Church of Scotland is ecumenically involved in sharing in the development of church and society in contemporary China – something which few can doubt to be of momentous significance in future world history. It is a post-imperial, post-missionary, post-denominational form of involvement and one that is enriching and challenging for the Church of Scotland itself.

Two very particular expressions of the importance attached by the Church of Scotland to its partner church relations are to be found in moderatorial visits, and in the participation of delegates and visitors from around the world in the General Assembly.

In recent years the moderatorial programme has included two major overseas tours, carried out at the request of the Board of World Mission. These are, essentially, visits to partner churches and signify, at the highest level, the seriousness with which the Church of Scotland takes the particular relationship in question. My own moderatorial travels took me to south-east Asia (Sri Lanka, Singapore and Burma), to the Middle East (Lebanon, Syria and Egypt) and to Canada. The first two of these tours were undertaken at the behest of the Board of World Mission. The visit to Canada was in response to an invitation from the Presbyterian Church in Canada in connection with particular celebrations which called for a presence from 'the old country'. The variety and extent of partner church links can be seen from the moderatorial visits of recent years. These have included Jamaica, Cuba, Malawi, Mozambique, Zambia, Nigeria, Kenya, Uganda, Sudan, South Africa, Australia, New Zealand, India, Thailand, South Korea and China.

Each of my own visits said something significant about the value of partnership. In Sri Lanka, Singapore and Burma we had rich contacts with the churches at the level of governance and administration and also with local congregations. In Singapore I preached to a large and youthful congregation at Sunday worship, gave a lecture in one of the major theological colleges in the region and engaged in discussions with officials of the Presbyterian Church on issues of church government and polity. In Sri Lanka we saw at first hand the practical, caring work of the National Council of Churches in response to the devastation caused by civil war. I preached and celebrated Communion in the Scots Kirk, St Andrew's, Colombo, which was established by Scottish tea planters in the 1840s. I also preached at the weekly Communion service in the Theological College of Lanka in Kandy, where our mission partner, the Reverend Tony McLean-Foreman, was a member of the teaching staff, and saw, at first hand, work being done through a women's project, supported by the Church of Scotland, to give life skills to young people suffering from mental incapacity, who had been rejected by their families. In Burma the very fact of our visit signalled solidarity with churches facing 'serious issues of conflict' (to quote again from the Board of World Mission's 2003 report). We were deeply moved by the quiet courage and dignity with which the people of that beautiful country cope with life under a nasty and brutal military regime. Many British men and women, including my own father, saw active service in Burma during the Second World War, and the links between our two countries were also underlined during the course of a private meeting with Aung San Suu Kyi, a meeting arranged by the British Embassy, during which she spoke affectionately of her connection, through her late husband's family, with Grantown-on-Spey.

Our visit to Lebanon, Syria and Egypt took place as war in Iraq was looking inevitable and imminent – which indeed it was. There is no denying the fact that the churches in the region are under pressure, particularly the Protestant (also known as Evangelical) churches. The perception of many Muslims is that the 'Christian' west is the enemy: the failure of the great western powers to deliver a just and lasting solution to the Israel/Palestine conflict and the decision to go to war in Iraq tended to confirm rather than alter that perception. It was therefore regarded as a powerful gesture of support that the most senior official of the Church of Scotland should pay a visit to the churches in the region, and take the opportunity of engaging in friendly dialogue with both Christian and Muslim communities. In recognition of the office of Moderator, a recurring feature of all our overseas visits was High Commission or Embassy hospitality, often in the form of a dinner which brought leaders of the different faith communities together. In Colombo, Rangoon, Beirut and Damascus such occasions proved both enjoyable and (we were told) highly useful to the local participants. In Egypt, too, we were warmly welcomed, not least in Asiyut, the Upper Egypt Presbyterian heartland, but also an area where Christians have suffered violence at the hands of Islamic extremists. We heard also of delays and frustrations experienced by churches in trying to get planning consent for work on their buildings, simply because they were churches, and of a minister who nearly went to prison for losing patience and having the work done without permission. In Cairo we saw the work of Church of Scotland mission partners, Drs Keith and Lai Russell, with Christian Sudanese refugees, fleeing vicious persecution by Islamic fundamentalists in the south of that country. One young man showed us the scars of torture endured for speaking out against the iniquity of female genital mutilation. We could do no more than listen and weep and pray, but did take some comfort from the fact the Church of Scotland was involved in providing him with some practical care and support.

On the other side of the world our time in Canada demonstrated the Church's global reach through emigration, as distinct from mission. The trigger for the visit was a long-standing request that the Moderator of the day should preach at the bi-centennial celebrations of the Church of St Andrew and St Paul in Montreal. As the name suggests this congregation, like many in Scotland, represents a union and both component parts were established by early Scots settlers. Indeed, I was intrigued when reading the history of the church to discover that echoes of the nineteenth-century Scottish controversies, such as the Disruption, were to reverberate through the church in Canada. Our travels also took us to St Andrew's churches in Ottawa and in Calgary where we met many Scots – some fairly recent arrivals, others who had come to Canada straight from school or university and settled, and others again whose parents or grandparents had emigrated. The Presbyterian and United Churches in Canada are now highly diverse in terms of ethnicity and culture, but the ties to Scotland and the Church of Scotland remain strong.

The other powerful expression of partner church relationships comes in the General Assembly. For many years the tradition has been that on the Sunday evening of the Assembly delegates and visitors from other churches are welcomed and greeted by the Moderator. This ceremony is both ecumenical and international. In 2003 the ecumenical delegates came from the Presbyterian Churches in Ireland and Wales, the United Reformed Church, the Baptist and Methodist Churches, the Church of England, the Roman Catholic Church, the Salvation Army, the Scottish Episcopal Church, the United Free Church and the Congregational Federation. The Ecumenical Bodies – Action of Churches Together in Scotland (ACTS), Churches Together in Britain and Ireland (CTBI) and the Conference of European Churches (CEC) – were also represented. From other countries around the world came church representatives from Ghana, Kenya, Malawi, Zimbabwe, Sudan, India, Pakistan, South Korea, Burma, Singapore, Sri Lanka, Jamaica, the Czech Republic, France, Germany, Italy, the Netherlands, Poland, Ukraine, Egypt, Palestine, Syria, Lebanon, Canada, New Zealand and Australia. In addition greetings from partner churches unable to attend were sent from Mozambique, Zambia, Bangladesh, Nepal, Thailand, Trinidad and Tobago, Austria, Croatia, Denmark, Finland, Norway, Germany, Hungary, Lithuania, Luxembourg, Portugal, Romania, Sweden, Switzerland, Ukraine, the United States of America and the Philippines.

I have always found the reception of delegates and visitors from around the world to be a most moving and significant moment in the General Assembly. It underlines the reality that the Church is a truly global network with disciples of Jesus Christ in every nation under the sun. This perspective is supremely important and sets the General Assembly in its proper context. While much of the Assembly's business has to do with the work of the Church in Scotland it is also the case that the Church is part of the one, holy, catholic and apostolic Church, and what it is and what it does is, therefore, part of the whole body of Christ in the world. Those who come officially from other churches with the status of 'delegate' are permitted to speak in the General Assembly and many do, both by bringing greetings and by taking part in debates. 'Visitors' from other churches are not entitled to speak, but are welcomed along with the official delegates, given facilities enabling them to attend the Assembly sessions and included in various social events and fringe gatherings. The Church of Scotland has not gone as far as the United Reformed Church in its recognition of those who come from other churches. On two occasions I have been the official delegate from the Church of Scotland to the URC Assembly where I was accorded the privilege, as were delegates from some other churches, of being a full voting member of that Assembly. The rationale, it was explained to me, was that this was a very practical way of allowing the universal Church to be part of a denominational decision-making process.

WINDS OF CHANGE

The Church of Scotland has a long tradition of offering comment on international affairs. The report of the Church and Nation Committee each year contains a section under this heading with sections in recent years covering countries as diverse as Zimbabwe, Iraq, Israel/Palestine, Kosovo, Bosnia, South Africa, Rwanda, East Timor, Malawi, Cambodia and Burma. Such reports are invariably well researched, providing an invaluable resource for church members and others, seeking to be better informed on international issues, and also providing the General Assembly with the opportunity of making comment to the UK government and governments abroad. It has been suggested that, with the advent of the Scottish Parliament, the significance of the General Assembly, once regarded as Scotland's 'unofficial parliament' would diminish. It is too early to assess the accuracy of this prediction but, in view of the fact that foreign policy is a reserved matter, the Assembly's voice in this area remains relevant, significant and welcome.

It is especially worth noting the degree of seriousness with which the General Assembly was involved in the debates of the 1950s and 1960s concerning the transition of former British colonies into independent countries. In particular the Church's support for the principle of majority rule in the creation of the Central African Federation, and the subsequent crisis over Southern Rhodesia, was both consistent and crucial. In 1952, for example, the General Assembly, commenting on the constitutional proposals for federation, urged 'that full consideration be given to African opinion and that no scheme should be adopted without the consent and co-operation of the Africans'.[11] By 1958 the Assembly had decided to appoint a Special Committee anent Central Africa, convened by the Very Reverend Dr George MacLeod, later to become Lord MacLeod of Fuinary, and this Committee reported annually, and at some length, over the next five years. Given the missionary record of the Church of Scotland in the region, the depth of knowledge and experience reflected in the detailed analysis of the issues, and the stature of those who spoke for the Church, these reports, with their consistent calls for justice, freedom and opportunity for all, carried great authority both in London and in Africa itself. They reflect well on the Church of Scotland and its global reach. Echoes of these debates were heard again in the General Assembly of 1992 when the Church's voice had a significant political impact in Malawi in terms of de-legitimising the regime of Hastings Banda.[12]

Similarly the Assembly's steady opposition to apartheid in South Africa was a powerful witness, and a credible force in leading to the dismantling of that vile system in 1990. From the mid-1970s to the mid-1990s the Church and Nation Committee reported annually on developments in that country. For example, in 1986 the General Assembly passed a series of resolutions calling for an end to investment in South Africa, calling on the Thatcher government to impose targeted sanctions approved by the EEC and (echoing the Assembly of 1952) urging the government of South Africa 'to move towards giving their rightful place in the government of their country to the black majority'.[13] Scottish churchmen and women visited South Africa regularly to give moral and practical support and, when a senior delegation from the Reformed Presbyterian Church in Southern Africa visited Scotland in 1993, it paid tribute to the solidarity expressed by Scottish Christians to the anti-apartheid struggle, and in particular to the Woman's Guild.[14] Professor Kenneth Ross, General Secretary of the Board of World Mission, tells of his first visit to the Eastern Cape in 2000 and hearing Bongani Finca waxing eloquent about how much strength his people drew for the struggle against apartheid from the Guild's decision to encourage its members to boycott South African oranges. There were tears in his eyes as he recalled that act of solidarity.

That same year the Reverend Alan McDonald joined the Ecumenical Monitoring Programme: South Africa, set up as part of the effort to eliminate politically motivated violence, and the following year, 1994, when elections were held, the Reverend Maxwell Craig and Mrs Mary Miller acted as election monitors sent out by the Council of Churches of Britain and Ireland. During the course of the General Assembly of 1994 a special service was held in Greyfriars Tolbooth and Highland Kirk 'in recognition of this momentous time in South Africa' and of the fact that 'the transition to democracy and a civil society is difficult and costly'.[15]

HIV/AIDS PROJECT

We have already noted the concern of the Board of World Mission that, at a time when the Church of Scotland was prioritising its work, efforts should be made to find ways in which meaningful solidarity with partner churches in needy and strife-torn countries could be expressed. One very practical expression of this concern was the approval given by the General Assembly of 2002 to a special project focusing on HIV/AIDS. The aim was to raise awareness in congregations about the impact of HIV/AIDS and to seek to channel urgently needed support to partner churches. The privilege of launching this important, life-saving initiative fell to me during the course of my moderatorial year.

The scale of the epidemic, more accurately described as a 'pandemic', was set out in the Board of World Mission's report to the General Assembly of 2002. Identified by Nelson Mandela as 'a tragedy of unprecedented proportions', it affects 40 million infected people world wide, over 28 million of them in sub-Saharan Africa. It is difficult to take in such enormous numbers, but one shocking statement of the scale of the crisis has pointed out that the number of people projected to die of AIDS over the next ten years (70 million) is the equivalent of six twin towers disasters every day for the next ten years. We have seen the (understandable) response of the United States to the twin towers atrocity and we affirm the value of every life lost on 11 September 2001. The challenge now is to attach an equivalent value to the lives of those threatened by poverty and disease world wide. The Church of Scotland's HIV/AIDS project is one response to that challenge.

The Project is about raising money in order to provide practical, caring help to partner churches, especially in sub-Saharan Africa and other chronically affected areas. However, it is also about 'breaking the silence' and educating people at home. The Board's 2002 report acknowledged that the Church had not always found it easy to talk about AIDS in ways that were not judgemental. The report tells of a World AIDS day service in the Roman Catholic Cathedral in Bujumbura in 1995 in which the priest said, in the course of his sermon, 'We must have compassion for people with AIDS, because they have sinned and because they are suffering for it now.' At that point a woman called Jeanne Gapiya rose (Jenny Geddes style), walked to the front of the church and announced: 'I have HIV, and I am a faithful wife. Who are you to say that I have sinned, or that you have not? We are all sinners, which is just as well, because it is for us that Jesus came.' Out of that moment, the report records, there grew the Burundi Association of Seropositive People. Burundi is a long way from Scotland, but we have seen in this chapter how small the world is and how connected the Church of Scotland is with every part of the world. It is estimated, for example, that members of the Church of Scotland, over and above their offerings for the work of the Church, give upwards of £1million annually to Christian Aid. It is to that same kindly spirit of generosity and concern for the very poorest and most vulnerable of people that the HIV/AIDS project appeals.

At the end of the day, perhaps any tension between affirming the priority of local churches in Scotland, as the Assembly Council and *Church without Walls* have done, and remembering the Church's commitment to labour for the advancement of the kingdom of God in all the world, is more imagined than real. One vital aspect of the work of the Board of World Mission has to do with local involvement. This means ensuring that local congregations are kept informed about the church overseas and given a sense of the church which is both local and global. Many congregations are only too happy to develop a relationship with individual mission partners who maintain correspondence and visit when home on leave. Sometimes such relationships will be translated into practical, financial support for specific projects like sinking a well or helping equip a school or hospital. The awakening of such awareness and concern for all God's people is an essential element in ensuring that the gospel story continues to be told and lived out in Scotland, and in nurturing worshipping and witnessing communities.

NOTES

1 Assembly Reports, 1985, p. 105.
2 Assembly Reports, 1995, p. 106.
3 The Council as reformed in 1996 – see Chapter 2.
4 John A. Duke, *The History of the Church of Scotland to the Reformation,* London: Oliver & Boyd, 1937, p. 111.
5 See J. H. S. Burleigh, *A Church History of Scotland,* London: Oxford University Press, 1960, p. 128.
6 James Bulloch and Andrew Drummond, *The Scottish Church 1688–1843,* Edinburgh: Saint Andrew Press, 1973, p. 151.
7 T. M. Devine, *The Scottish Nation 1700–2000,* London: Allen Lane, 1999, p. 470.
8 Reports to the General Assembly, 1926, p. 712.
9 See *Church of Scotland Year Book, 2003–2004,* Edinburgh: Saint Andrew Press, p. 35.
10 Assembly Reports, 2003, p. 26/1.

11 Assembly Reports, 1952, p. 331.
12 See Kenneth R. Ross, 'Malawi's Peaceful Revolution 1992–94: The Role of the Church of Scotland', *Scottish Church History Society Records*, XXVII (1997), pp. 280–304.
13 Collated Deliverance, General Assembly, 1986, p. 8.
14 See Assembly Reports, Church and Nation Committee, 1994, p. 230.
15 See Assembly Reports, Church and Nation Committee, 1994, p. 231.

4

The Changing Face of the General Assembly

SOME HISTORICAL BACKGROUND

'Take from us the freedom of Assemblies and take from us the Evangel; for without Assemblies, how shall good order and unity of doctrine be kept?' These words, commonly attributed to John Knox, underline the importance attached by the Reformers of coming together to consider the life and witness of the Church. It is also important to note that Knox's comment was made in response to a question raised in the General Assembly of 1561, namely, whether meetings of the General Assembly could be held without the consent of the Sovereign. Knox's answer made it clear that they should, they could and they would!

The first General Assembly was held in December 1560 and comprised forty-one members, of which six were ministers. The others present, according to Professor J. H. S. Burleigh, were 'some lairds and representatives of towns'.[1] Dr Stewart Mechie, in his book *The Office of Lord High Commissioner*, makes the point that the General Assembly 'was not at this period a purely ecclesiastical body ... but was rather more like an ecclesiastical version of the estates of the realm, the membership consisting of superintendents[2] and ministers together with barons and representatives of burghs'. Dr Mechie notes that certain burghs continued to send commissioners to the General Assembly up to 1929[3] and still, today, representatives of every Scottish local authority attend the formal opening of the Assembly.

Knox's principle of freedom of assembly was fiercely contested in the decades following the Reformation. The Stuart kings (James VI and I, Charles I and Charles II) all preferred Episcopalianism to

Presbyterianism. Putting it bluntly, it was easier to control the Church through bishops than through presbytery or General Assembly. James remarked, famously, 'no bishop, no king' and 'a Scots presbytery agreeth as well with monarchy as God with the devil'. In seventeenth-century England there was political tension between Parliament and Crown; in Scotland the tension was between the Presbyterian Kirk and the Crown. That said, the king regularly attended meetings of the General Assembly, taking part in the business. At the same time he sought to 'manage' the Assembly by ensuring that those upon whom he could rely were present. Despite Knox's assertions over freedom of Assembly the king would have no scruples about changing the previously agreed time and place of the next meeting. For example, a General Assembly held in Dundee in 1598 resolved to meet the next year in Aberdeen, but, following the king's intervention, the meeting took place in Montrose in 1600. Eventually, James' control was complete and the Assemblies of 1606 to 1618 obligingly enacted a series of Episcopalian measures, including the reappointment of bishops and a requirement that church members kneel at communion.

After 1618 the Assembly did not meet again until 1638. This was the year of the signing of the National Covenant[4] and the year after a woman called Jenny Geddes is reported to have thrown her stool at the minister in St Giles', in protest at the imposition of an Anglican prayer book ('Durst thou say mass in my lug?'). Feelings were certainly running high when, in 1638, the General Assembly met in Glasgow Cathedral. Indeed, the gathering has been likened to the French National Assembly of 1789. Revolution was in the air and it was not long before the King's Commissioner, the Marquis of Hamilton, dissolved the Assembly and withdrew. However, the Assembly declined to be dissolved and proceeded to annul the decisions of what it called 'the pretended Assemblies' of 1606 to 1618. It is an indication of the political turmoil of the times that, fifteen years later, the Clerk of the Glasgow Assembly, Archibald Johnston of Warriston, was executed for treason – a fate (I trust) unlikely to befall an Assembly Clerk today!

In 1690 Presbyterianism was established as the settled form of government of the Church of Scotland, with the legal recognition of a separate Scottish Episcopal Church following in 1712. However, the spiritual independence of the Church was to remain an issue for another two centuries, resulting, as we have seen, in secession and disruption. Such matters as the right of a congregation to choose its own minister and the freedom of the Church to determine its own doctrine continued to be fought for.

THE LORD HIGH COMMISSIONER

There is a formality and a ceremonial surrounding the opening of the General Assembly which some question. In particular, it has been argued, for example by Harry Reid in *Outside Verdict*, that the office of Lord High Commissioner ought to be laid decently to rest.[5] The argument is that the panoply surrounding the role gives the wrong signals in the twenty-first century and suggests a link between Church and State which is no longer appropriate. This is an understandable point of view and one with which many will agree. On the other hand, the office does offer an important reminder of our history as a national church, and once such traditions are abolished they have gone forever. By continuing the office, with an appropriate level of ceremonial, we are recalling the great struggles between Church and Crown and celebrating the happy constitutional accommodation at which we have now arrived, namely, a national recognition of religion combined with the spiritual independence of the Church.

In this connection, it is both interesting and instructive to compare the different arrangements which apply to the Church of England and the Church of Scotland in such matters. The Sovereign is supreme governor of the Church of England and bishops are appointed by the Prime Minister on the basis that twenty-six of them have seats in the House of Lords. By contrast, the Sovereign has no constitutional role in the Church of Scotland and, when in Scotland, while welcomed and received with appropriate dignity, worships simply as a member of the congregation.

The present Queen has attended General Assemblies in 1960, 1969, 1977 and 2002, and, like her predecessors, is represented in her absence by a Lord High Commissioner. It is important to stress that the Sovereign's function is simply to attend and address the Assembly. It is quite wrong to say, as a number of media reports in 2002 did, that the Queen, when present, opens the General Assembly. Convention also dictates that the Sovereign or Lord High Commissioner does not enter the Assembly Hall itself, but sits in a throne gallery overlooking the Hall. Protocol prescribes that the Lord High Commissioner be treated as though he or she were the Sovereign and be accorded the courtesy title 'Your Grace'. Recent royal Lords High Commissioner (Princess Anne in 1996 and Prince Charles in 2000) used this ancient title rather than 'Your Royal Highness'. In terms of precedence, while the Assembly is sitting, the Lord High Commissioner ranks next to the Sovereign and the Duke of Edinburgh and before the rest of the royal family. Appropriate courtesies apply. Much hilarity was occasioned in 1999 when an over-zealous traffic warden, no doubt with an eye to a different kind of commission, attempted to 'book' the Lord High Commissioner's car as it waited outside the Edinburgh International Conference Centre. In the altercation which ensued with the royal chauffeur, the traffic warden was heard to say, 'And what's more, I'm booking you for not having a number plate.'

As the first few paragraphs of this chapter indicate, the relationship between Crown and Assembly has not always been as cordial as it is today. In the past the king himself, or his Commissioner, was not above taking part in the debate. Stewart Michie, in the book already referred to, tells that in 1726 the Commissioner actually proposed a candidate for Moderator, who was, in fact, elected by a small majority.[6] In 1752, the General Assembly, which had to deal with a case of a presbytery refusing to induct the patron's nominee to a charge because he was not acceptable to the people[7] was told, in no uncertain terms by the Lord High Commissioner (the Earl of Leven), that 'it was time it exerted its authority firmly over inferior courts'. Lord Reith also came close to lecturing the Assembly as recently as 1968 when he instructed the Assembly 'to believe the eternal verities of the Gospel'. There have even been cases where the Lord High Commissioner was also a regular commissioner to the General Assembly. This happened in 1910 when the Earl of Stair had already been elected a commissioner by his presbytery when appointed Lord High Commissioner. Some thought that he would resign his presbytery commission, but he did not and, on one occasion, left the throne gallery to contribute to a debate from within the Assembly.

A pleasing and useful custom is the tradition of the Lord High Commissioner having guests to stay overnight at Holyrood, who then attend the General Assembly the following morning. Where a particularly distinguished guest is present, the convention is that the Business Convener draws the Moderator's attention to their presence, and proposes that the guest be invited to address the Assembly. By this means the Chief Rabbi, the Archbishop of Canterbury, the Chancellor of the Exchequer, the Speaker of the House of Commons, the UK Representative of the Palestinian Authority and the Prime Minister of the day have all addressed the Assembly in recent years. It is important, and helpful, to remember that these are not the Assembly's invited guests, but the Lord High Commissioner's. For example, in 1988, after Prime Minister Margaret Thatcher addressed the Assembly, the question was raised as to whether, in the interest of political balance, an invitation should be sent the following year to the Leader of the Opposition. The answer was that the Prime Minister was the Lord High Commissioner's guest to whom the Assembly had extended a courtesy, appropriate to her office. There was no question of the Church itself extending such an invitation.

Bearing in mind Knox's 1561 call for freedom of Assembly it is worth remarking that up until 1926 the Lord High Commissioner concluded his farewell address to the General Assembly with the words, 'In virtue of the powers vested in me by His Majesty the King, I now dissolve this Assembly in the king's name and appoint that the next Assembly shall meet on . . .' Not surprisingly, this was an issue for the union then being negotiated between the Church of Scotland and the United Free Church. So it came about that the following year, 1927, a new formula was introduced. The Lord High Commissioner that year, the Earl of Stair, concluded his farewell address with the words: 'I shall inform His Majesty that having concluded the business for which you assembled you have passed an Act appointing your next meeting to be held on . . . and now in the king's name, I bid you farewell'. This form of words is used to the present day, with one of the final pieces of business despatched by the Assembly being the passing of an Act appointing the date of the next General Assembly.

THE ASSEMBLY AS IT HAS DEVELOPED IN MODERN TIMES

The General Assembly is the highest of the three courts of the Church of Scotland, the other two being the Kirk Session and the presbytery. Until 1992 there was a fourth court, the synod, which was intermediate between the presbytery and the General Assembly. However, synods had become increasingly superfluous to the Church's government. Invariably, matters appealed to the synod from the presbytery continued to the General Assembly for final judgement. Synod meetings were poorly attended and there was a sense that there was no real business for the court.

By custom the General Assembly meets in Edinburgh on the third Saturday of May in the Assembly Hall. The Hall was built for the General Assembly of the Free Church within New College and first used in 1859. The Established Church Assembly Hall was immediately adjacent in the Lawnmarket, in what is now the Edinburgh Festival Centre, also known as The Hub. Following the 1929 union the decision was taken to use the Free Church Hall for meetings of the General Assembly of the united Church.

In 1999 the Hall became the temporary home of the Scottish Parliament, the lease requiring the Parliament to vacate the Hall for three weeks in May to allow the General Assembly to meet at its accustomed time. This arrangement, negotiated between civil servants and church officials, prior to the election of the Parliament, seemed a sensible and economical sharing of the Hall, the thought being that for the three weeks in question the Parliament might operate in committee, rather than plenary. In the event, the Parliament, once it came into being, took a different view and wished to continue its day and a half a week of plenary meetings throughout May. Co-operatively, the Church agreed to waive the terms of the lease in 1999 and 2001, the Assembly meeting in those years in the Edinburgh International Conference Centre and the Usher Hall, respectively. In 2000 the Parliament moved, temporarily, to Glasgow and in 2002 to Aberdeen. While there were some grumblings about the cost, this moving of the Parliament was warmly welcomed in the west and the north-east.

The first General Assembly I attended as a commissioner was in 1972, a year after my ordination. The Moderator that year was the Right Reverend Dr Ronald Selby Wright, Minister of the Canongate Kirk in Edinburgh. I recall Dr Selby Wright, in his acceptance speech, acknowledging that, during the course of his ministry, he had not been much involved in the affairs of the General Assembly. He did recall asking a question a number of years previously, for which he was still awaiting an answer! Another memory of that 'first-impression' Assembly is how very male it was in composition. After all, it was just four years since women had been admitted to the ministry and six years since they had become eligible for the eldership.

At that time the Assembly opened on a Tuesday morning and continued until the Wednesday of the following week. The first event was a service in St Giles' after which the commissioners made their way up the Lawnmarket and took their places in the Assembly Hall. In 1978 the pattern now followed was introduced. The Assembly convenes in the Assembly Hall on the third Saturday of May and concludes the following Friday evening. This shorter duration was brought about partly on financial grounds but also in the hope that containing the Assembly within one working week would make it easier for younger, working elders to attend. Under the new arrangements the Assembly Communion service was moved from St Giles' to the Assembly Hall, one of the arguments being that it was highly appropriate to celebrate the sacrament in the place of work and business.

The style and function of the General Assembly was one of the topics addressed by the Committee of Forty. In its 1976 report the Committee quoted from the record of the first Assembly of 1560 which stated that the meeting was 'convened to consult upon those things which are to set forward God's glory and the "weel" of his kirk in the realm'.[8] The

Committee considered that this purpose still applied and went on to break it down into four main areas, namely:

1. Policy, in which lines of action are authorised,
2. Doctrinal, in which doctrine is considered and formulated,
3. Judicial, in which cases are resolved,
4. Advisory, on which points of view are expressed and God's will for his people is sought.

The Committee further remarked that, in relation to (1) the lower courts of Kirk Session and presbytery had freedom within the policy outlines defined. Decisions under (2) and (3) were binding (subject to liberty of opinion in respect of doctrinal matters, not of the substance of the faith). Matters debated and decided under (4) were not binding in the same way. For example, church members were free to disagree with pronouncements of the General Assembly on matters such as nuclear weapons and abortion.

In reviewing the operation of the General Assembly the Committee put forward some radical ideas, with different models of how the Assembly and its committees might operate. Suggestions included a reduction in membership from 1,300 to around 500, the possibility of individuals being commissioned for four years rather than just one and the General Assembly meeting every other year, with greater use being made of a scaled-down Commission of Assembly[9] in between. These ideas were sent to presbyteries for their consideration, but found little favour across the Church.

There the matter rested until the General Assembly of 1994, when the Presbytery of Kirkcaldy brought an Overture, asking that the Assembly Council undertake a review of the General Assembly. This review, it was envisaged, would cover 'the structure, size, system of representation, duration and cost' and also such matters as how frequently boards reported and the way judicial cases were dealt with. The General Assembly approved the Overture, though gave the remit not to the Assembly Council as suggested but to the Board of Practice and Procedure, the body with responsibility for Assembly arrangements. Over the next two years the Board engaged in a thorough and radical review of the Assembly, in consultation with presbyteries and through a series of meetings around the country. Out of this process a number of proposals for change were brought to the Assembly of 1996 along with an indication of certain areas where change was not being recommended.

Change was recommended in the following areas:

1. The Assembly should be reduced in size by an adjustment of the formula for appointing ministers from one in three to one in four. This would reduce the number of commissioners from 1,120 to 870. The Board resisted further reduction on the grounds that it would severely reduce the frequency with which individual ministers attended.

2. Pre-report briefings by committees should be encouraged as a way of enabling commissioners to become better informed about the issues for debate, and perhaps also to reduce the number of questions put in the Assembly itself.

3. Conference sessions should be introduced from time to time, allowing for a less formal discussion of an issue than is possible under normal Assembly procedures.

4. Over and above their allocation of commissioners, each presbytery should be invited to send a youth representative between the ages of eighteen and twenty-five who would have the status of a corresponding member (that is, be allowed to speak but not vote).

5. The Commission of Assembly should be reconstituted as a body comprising one-tenth of the commissioners to the preceding Assembly. This would give a membership of around eighty. The Commission would meet as required and would deal with matters, such as appeals over readjustment matters, thereby relieving pressure on the Assembly timetable, and also allowing for fuller and more detailed consideration of such cases.

6. The week-long Assembly, introduced in 1978, should continue, but the week should run from a Thursday until the following

Wednesday. This would allow the Assembly to get straight down to business and could also be helpful from a media point of view.

7. Reporting by boards should be streamlined. An aim of reducing the length of written reports by 50 per cent was mentioned, as was the idea of an executive summary included with longer reports. Reports should be in two sections, the first part reporting diligence, the second proposing policy or action for approval. Only the latter should have a deliverance (specific recommendations) attached.

8. Moderators should be encouraged to develop Assembly worship beyond the traditional unaccompanied psalm singing.

Change was not recommended in the following areas:

1. The Assembly should continue to meet in the Assembly Hall in Edinburgh. Consultation had shown that only four presbyteries favoured the idea of the Assembly moving around the country. The status quo was favoured, largely on the grounds of convenience of travel and availability of accommodation. The Assembly Hall was there, so why go to the expense of hiring outside venues?

2. The Assembly should not become residential, as some had suggested. The wish to meet annually in the Assembly Hall meant that complicated and costly transport arrangements to and from the place of residence would be required. It was also noted that many central-Scotland-based commissioners preferred to travel from home daily.

3. Proposals to hold the Assembly at a time other than May were looked at, but not taken forward. In a matter such as this it was recognised that there was no pleasing everyone. Some favoured a shift to September so that the Assembly could set the tone for the new session. Others argued that the start of a new session was not a good time for ministers attending the Assembly to be away from their congregations.

4. The possibility of the Assembly meeting every two years came up again and, again, did not find favour. Practical considerations,

such as the lengthening of Barrier Act procedures and a two-year Moderatorship were adduced, but more generally the Board also noted that 'the Church looks annually to the General Assembly for something hard to define, yet real in terms of identity'.

5. Comment had been made on the fact that a number of individuals seemed to attend the General Assembly every year and took 'an undue part in its deliberations'. It had been suggested that a limit be set on the number of times an individual could speak, and that presbytery clerks should have a new 'observer status'. (These two were not necessarily connected!) Against such suggestions the Board stressed that the choice of commissioners was a matter for presbyteries and that it would be constitutionally invidious to limit this right. Nevertheless, presbyteries were urged, as far as possible, to appoint different commissioners each year. Certainly, my own experience, as far as too frequent speakers are concerned, is that the Assembly has its own ways of making its feelings known when someone rises to speak once too often!

6. There had also been a suggestion that boards should not be required to report annually, but on a rotational basis. This would allow them to devote time to real work, as distinct from preparing reports, and also give more time for individual debates in the Assembly. However, on examining this idea in detail it emerged that there were practical difficulties in its implementation and, in any case, the Assembly was entitled to call its agencies to account whenever it met.

The following year (1997) the Board reported that, with one exception, all of its proposals for change had found favour with a majority of presbyteries. The exception was the suggestion that the Assembly run from Thursday to Wednesday, rather than from Saturday to Friday. The containment of the Assembly within the working week, as had been argued in 1978, was still felt to make things easier for working elders. There had also been wide approval of the recommendations on matters which should not be altered.

The changes adopted in this most recent review have contributed significantly to the modernisation of the General Assembly, which feels a very different body from that which I attended as a first-time commissioner in 1972. As noted, that consisted almost entirely of men and, while there was much good humour, there was also more formality than today. Male ministerial conveners invariably wore frock coat, clerical collar and striped trousers when presenting their reports and the same dress code applied to the convener and vice-convener of the Business Committee. Today, dress is somewhat more relaxed, though (on the whole) still appropriate to the dignity of the court.

Changes in worship have been welcomed by many. The traditional unaccompanied psalm singing remains as a much-loved start to the day, and visitors invariably remark upon it as a highlight of the week. However, the Assembly has a mind of its own. On one occasion the Moderator announced Psalm 23 to the tune 'Orlington'. Now, the opening bars of 'Orlington' are very similar to the more familiar tune 'Wiltshire'. By verse 3 'Wiltshire' had clearly won! A similar thing happened another year between the tunes 'Caithness' and 'St Paul' for the sixtieth paraphrase ('Father of peace, and God of Love'). Today the psalms are supplemented by hymns, traditional and contemporary. Soloists have been used and, instead of the Scripture being read by one of the clerks, a variety of voices has been heard from commissioners and delegates (both ecumenical and overseas). A Gaelic reading is also regularly included. In 2000 the Moderator, the Right Reverend Andrew McLellan, arranged for a radio link to a mission partner in Malawi, a country he was to visit later in the year. At the appropriate point in the proceedings the voice of Carol Finlay was heard loud, clear and live from Ekwendeni Hospital. Dr McLellan's predecessor, the Right Reverend John Cairns, introduced an African Children's Choir from Sudan and, in my own year as Moderator (2002), to mark the Year of the Child, children led some of the prayers one morning. Whatever else it is or does, the General Assembly should be a place where people find inspiration. One obvious place to look for that inspiration is in the worship and my sense is that people have not been disappointed.

The arrival of youth representatives has also brought refreshment. Initially, the rule was that they could speak but neither vote nor move a motion. It was not long, however, before a device emerged whereby the youth 'rep' would find a friendly and sympathetic commissioner who would formally move the motion, leaving them free to make the proposing speech. If you can't beat them, join them(!), and in time the Board of Practice and Procedure recommended, and the Assembly agreed, that youth representatives should be permitted to propose motions in their own right, though still not to vote. This latter restriction arises from the constitutional consideration that full voting membership of the General Assembly belongs to ministers, elders and deacons commissioned for the purpose by presbyteries. Nevertheless, the youth representatives have become very much part of the Assembly and have approached the role with a diligence that commissioners have both recognised and admired.

While referring to the youth representatives it is relevant to mention the Youth Assembly. This was held for the first time in April 1994 when approximately 250 young people met over two days in the Assembly Hall. Specially prepared reports were presented by selected Assembly conveners (National Mission, Social Responsibility, Parish Education, World Mission and Church and Nation) and these were then debated by the delegates. The Moderator of the day, Dr James Weatherhead, presided and I had the privilege of serving as clerk, with assistance from one of the young people (now a leading member of the Board of Stewardship and Finance!). Subsequent Youth Assemblies have been held around Scotland and the gathering has become a popular annual event. For the first time, the General Assembly of 2003 formally remitted some matters for consideration by the Youth Assembly due to meet later in the year.

In 2002 the youth representatives were joined by 'children's ambassadors'. In December 2001, the Board of Parish Education initiative 'The Year of the Child' was launched. This project, backed by the General Assembly, sought to emphasise the important place occupied by children within the life of the Church and to encourage the Church to listen to the children. To help facilitate this process 'Children's Forums' were established around the country and it was agreed that a small group of children should attend the opening few days of the General Assembly. I was particularly pleased that they were so positioned outside St Giles' after the Assembly service that they could exchange pleasantries with the Queen and the Duke of Edinburgh. With great laughter, one little boy told me afterwards that he had been amazed and delighted that the Queen appeared to know his name – then realised he was wearing a name badge! Clearly much of the Assembly business was of limited interest to the children and, mercifully, the Board of Parish Education had also arranged a programme of activities outwith the Hall. But there was no denying the thrill the children felt in being in the Assembly even for a limited time and helping the Moderator lead the opening worship one day. I still like to recall a petition from one child's prayer: 'We pray for the Moderator, Finlay Macdonald, that he may have a nice time.' I can tell that child that her prayer worked! Thank you.

The other innovation brought in in 1997 was the Conference Session. This provides for the general discussion of a topic, free from the formal procedures of the Assembly. The idea is to discuss something, without the pressure of reaching a decision through motions, counter-motions and amendments. This approach has been used when a presbytery meets in conference, with a view to increasing awareness and understanding of an issue, before going on to take a more formal view. The kind of subjects people had in mind, when suggesting this option, were issues raised by science and technology, which often moved so quickly that ethical and theological opinion struggled to keep up. The argument was that, rather than dividing the Assembly on a subject like cloning, the technicalities of which many people did not understand, it would be preferable to have a general discussion, led by some experts in the relevant field. A sufficient outcome would be a greater understanding of the issues. This might (or might not) lead in time to a formal debate, with proposed resolutions, designed to lead the General Assembly to a position on the matter.

This kind of conference session has not been taken up to any great extent, though in 1994 the General Assembly did decide to consider two conflicting reports on human sexuality in this kind of way. The Assembly resolved that the issues set out in the reports would be discussed but no substantive decisions made. Given the controversial nature of the subject the debate generated as much heat as light (probably more of the former) and many of those present found it a not particularly satisfactory experience. More successful were open evenings such as 'Sharing the Pain, Holding the Hope' (2002), which focused on life in urban priority areas, with contributions from local church members in drama, music and humour. In fact the success of this style of gathering has encouraged the growth of an Assembly 'fringe', with book-signings, lunch-time meetings on particular themes and singing sessions to introduce the new hymn book, to mention but a few. Another very popular innovation has been the pre-Assembly briefing for first-time commissioners. This not only provides practical information. It also facilitates introductions, with people arranging to meet up so that they can sit and socialise together. And in 1999, the year the Assembly was at the state-of-the-art Edinburgh International Conference Centre, a major car dealer even had a range of its models on display so that ministers could sign up for special offer car-leasing deals.

The Assembly has also moved forward through the use of modern technology. While commissioners are encouraged to give as much notice as possible of amendments, this is not always possible. Indeed, one of the remarkable things about the Assembly is that anyone, inspired by the debate to do so, may rise and propose a relevant motion. If the motion was long or complex, it used to be the case that commissioners had to rely on hearing it read to them. Now, with the use of computers, the motion appears on the screens, more or less immediately, for everyone to see. Commissioners are issued with swipe cards which are used for activating microphones, recording electronic votes, gaining access to the hall and even claiming expenses. Truly, the Assembly has moved with the times.

THE OFFICE OF MODERATOR

A topic to which the Church seems to return every few years is the election of the Moderator. The process used to be conducted with great secrecy and the theory was that the only name ever to emerge from the Nominating Committee's deliberations was that of the Moderator-elect. The reality was somewhat different with the next day's newspapers carrying reports which could have passed for minutes of the meeting. The system was opened up by new regulations introduced in 1999. These regulations, as adjusted in 2003, require that the names of those who have agreed to be nominated be made public two weeks before the meeting to nominate, and also that members of the Committee be furnished with biographical details in advance. The emphasis, however, remains on 'nomination' rather than 'candidacy' and there is no mechanism, as happens in some other churches, for the committee members to interview those under consideration. I recall arriving at the Presbyterian Church (USA) General Assembly in 1998 and being greeted by the three moderatorial candidates who, surrounded by their supporters, were canvassing the votes of commissioners. Each of them would address the Assembly later in the day, be subject to questioning, and then a vote would be taken to decide which one would be Moderator. There and then the successful candidate would take the chair.

The Church of Scotland Nominating Committee consists of a representative appointed by every presbytery (except Jerusalem), the three immediate past Moderators and three elders appointed by the General Assembly. Presumably where an elder has held the office, then a balancing minister will be required. In the General Assembly of 2002 there was a proposal that the method of appointing the committee should be re-examined with a view to guaranteeing a balance of age, gender, minister, elder, deacon etc. With each presbytery appointing its own representative the achievement of such a balance cannot be guaranteed. However, having so recently revised the regulations the Assembly was reluctant to make yet another change so soon.

The 1999 regulations also introduced an additional meeting of the Committee. Previously the Committee met 'cold' on the fourth Tuesday of October to consider nominations (of which no prior notice had been given) and vote upon them. Now there is an initial meeting in early September where broad consideration is given to the requirements of the Church. The outline programme for the next Moderator is tabled, with a note of the presbytery, overseas and other visits to be made. The three former Moderators give a brief presentation based on their experiences of serving as Moderator and members of the committee have an opportunity of reflecting together on the task entrusted to them. They are then charged with the task of approaching people whom they consider might do the job well. The three former Moderators may not propose or second nominees, though they do have a vote.

It is over four hundred years since an elder last served as Moderator of the General Assembly and until 2004 the office had never been held by a woman. This latter point has been the cause of some controversy in recent years. The nomination of Dr Alison Elliot, an elder and session clerk, to be Moderator of the 2004 General Assembly was thus doubly significant.

It is increasingly suggested that the Church would be better served were the Moderator to hold office for longer than one year. The arguments are based mainly on questions such as media profile which is more easily built up over a period of years. Under the present system, it cannot be denied, the Moderator is just becoming established when it is time to step down. In this way, it is argued, the Church of Scotland is put at a disadvantage compared with other churches whose leaders remain in post for a period of years.

This argument goes to the heart of Presbyterianism where leadership is a difficult concept. Whereas our sister church, the Church of England, views itself as having synodical government and episcopal leadership, the Church of Scotland simply has Presbyterian government. Leadership is not so clearly located. That is not to say that we lack leaders at local, regional and national level, but such leadership is exercised through the courts of the Church, constituted in the name of Jesus Christ, the King and Head of the Church, and under the guidance of the Holy Spirit. There is certainly an argument for the more personal leadership exercised by a bishop, but that is, by definition, something different from Presbyterianism.

Strictly speaking the Moderator of the General Assembly holds office, not for a year, but for a week, for, once the General Assembly is over there is nothing left to moderate. In practice, though, the Moderator goes forth from the Assembly as an ambassador, to exhort and encourage, to listen and to learn, to represent the General Assembly in congregational celebrations and on great occasions of State. The Moderator is frequently asked to make comment on issues of the day. In doing so he or she should have regard to decisions of the General Assembly and the views of its boards and committees. I have observed, however, that frequently the media, being attracted to the idea of a national leader, pay more attention to comment by the Moderator than to a statement by a convener or board. The last of the regulations governing the duties of Moderator, after listing specific tasks such as presiding at the General Assembly and visiting a number of presbyteries, gives a broad discretion 'to undertake such other duties as he [sic] may choose during his [sic] term of office'.[10] In exercise of this discretion Moderators are certainly able to give a lead in areas where they have particular interests, experience and competence, and this has been to the Church's benefit.

There are practical difficulties associated with a Moderator serving for more than one year. The present arrangements effectively involve seconding a minister from normal duties, and most congregations can cope with this for a year. To ask for a longer period of secondment would be unreasonable, and would involve the Moderator demitting his or her charge. Then, after their period of service (perhaps two, three, or five years) they would seek another appointment. However, there is a deeper issue to be addressed and that is precisely what does the Moderator do? I found myself describing the office as 'a role' rather than 'a job' – a wonderfully exciting and enriching role, but a role nevertheless. What I mean by this is that the Moderator moves from one thing to the next – preaching here, speaking there, visiting a factory, meeting community leaders –but does not become involved in a 'sleeves-rolled-up' kind of way, as one does in a normal job where there is continuity and responsibility. In fact, apart from chairing the General Assembly the Moderator has no real responsibilities in the way, for example, that a bishop does. Disgruntled people will write to the Moderator seeking intervention when a minister has declined to baptise a grandchild, but, of course the Moderator has no authority to do any such thing. If there is a genuine complaint against a minister, then it is a matter for the presbytery. That said, there is no denying the usefulness of the role in terms of giving encouragement within the Church at home, cementing relationships between the Church of Scotland and churches around the world and in terms of raising the profile of the church, locally and nationally.

On the question of length of tenure, however, I suggest that, were this to be extended beyond one year, then the Church would need to give the Moderator a more functional leadership role, combined with a measure of authority. The risk, though, is that people might quickly come to regard this as inconsistent with the principle of Presbyterian parity. Moreover, as I argued in an article on this subject in the October 2001 edition of *Life & Work*, if we pursue the episcopal comparison, the archbishop or the cardinal who is the functional head of his denomination is invariably supported by and drawn from a college of bishops who serve as regional denominational leaders. Consistency and good organisation, therefore, suggests that a Moderator, called to exercise real national leadership over a period of years, should be supported by a 'college' of full-time presbytery moderators. Indeed, if there is a real case for personal leadership at a national level, there is, arguably, an even stronger case for such leadership at presbytery level. The same arguments apply, after all. The local bishop will build up a profile in the local press and become known at local civic functions in a way that presbytery moderators will not.

Doubtless the debate will go on and perhaps one day we shall square the bishop/presbytery circle. It is interesting to recall that between 1560 and 1690 bishop and presbytery coexisted (though not very happily) within the one Church. After SCIFU the prospect does not feel particularly imminent, but, in God's good time, a day of happy reconciliation and reunion between the Kirk and the Scottish Episcopal Church, two very Scottish churches, may come.

NOTES

1 J. H. S. Burleigh, *A Church History of Scotland*, London: Oxford University Press, 1960, p. 178.
2 In the immediate aftermath of the Reformation superintendent ministers had responsibility for overseeing churches in a synod area.
3 Stewart Mechie, *The Office of Lord High Commissioner*, Edinburgh: Saint Andrew Press, 1957, p. 4.
4 The National Covenant, signed in Greyfriars Churchyard, 1638.
5 Harry Reid, *Outside Verdict*, Edinburgh: Saint Andrew Press, 2002.
6 Mechie, *Office of Lord High Commissioner*, p. 38.
7 The Inverkeithing case, which led to the deposition of Thomas Gillespie and the Second Secession.
8 Assembly Reports, 1976, p. 492.
9 The Commission of Assembly, at that time, was effectively the General Assembly meeting for a day in October, February and May to deal with delegated or urgent matters. In practice, only a minority of commissioners attended.
10 Revised Regulations governing the duties of the Moderator of the General Assembly, 1980.

5

Change and the Church's Worship

PSALMS, HYMNS AND SPIRITUAL SONGS

The liturgical historian, Millar Patrick, in his *Four Centuries of Scottish Psalmody* recounts a bizarre incident which occurred in Bridge of Teith Church in the eighteenth century. At that time only metrical psalms were sung in church services, and just twelve simple tunes were permitted. As no musical accompaniment was allowed the singing was led by a precentor. Some precentors were more innovative than others and the incident, from the 'days, when the tyranny of the Twelve Tunes still persisted' is as follows.

> New tunes [Millar Patrick writes] were beginning to be allowed elsewhere, and one day the precentor, without authorisation or warning, broke into the novel strains of Bangor when the psalm was given out. The minister, Mr Fletcher, sat for a moment or two dumbfounded, unable to believe his ears, then rose, seized the pulpit Bible and brought it down with stupefying force on the head of the offender beneath him, and dared him ever to be guilty of such an outrage again.[1]
>
> *Four Centuries of Scottish Psalmody* by Millar Patrick (1949). Reprinted by permission of Oxford University Press.

I learned many psalm tunes from my Hebridean grandmother, who used to come on extended visits to our home in Dundee. She was a great one for sewing and would spend hours at the treadle sewing machine, which shared a room with the piano. Formal practice of scales and Clementi over, I became a holy juke-box. Granny would call out her favourite psalm tunes and I would duly oblige with renditions of 'Dunfermline', 'Huddersfield', 'Martyrs' and many more – even the outrageous 'Bangor'! Forty years earlier she had been a strong supporter of the suffragette movement and now had a new cause. Between the psalm tunes she would wax eloquent on the iniquities of the Church's policy of barring women from the ministry and the eldership, and remind her teenage grandson that 'Women were the first apostles of the resurrection.' Still today I think of the psalm tunes by name and number, as they appeared in the old split-page psalter – 'Kilmarnock 75', 'French 61', 'Stroudwater 134'.

Millar Patrick also reminds us that the rendering of the psalms into metre and their setting to simple, easily remembered melodies was a vital element in the Scottish Reformation. The General Assembly, meeting in Edinburgh in December 1562, was clearly anxious to publish a selection of psalms for popular use, deciding to lend Robert Lekprevik, printer, 'twa hundreth punds to help buy irons, ink and paper and to fie craftsmen for printing'. Many tunes still much loved today, like 'Old Hundredth' and 'French', date from this period, some indigenous, others introduced from Strasbourg and Geneva. It was a nice touch when the Scottish Parliament, at its historic 'reconvening' on 1 July 1999, chose to mark the occasion with the singing of the 'Old Hundredth' – 'All people that on earth do dwell, sing to the Lord with cheerful voice'.[2]

Popular familiarity with the psalms also found expression in Burns' poem 'The Cottar's Saturday Night'. The poet writes with warm sentimentality of the family, gathered 'round the ingle' in domestic devotion:

> They chant their artless notes, in simple guise,
> They tune their hearts, by far the noblest aim;
> Perhaps 'Dundee's' wild-warbling measures rise,
> Or plaintive 'Martyrs', worthy of the name;
> Or noble 'Elgin' beets the heavenward flame,
> The sweetest far of Scotia's holy lays:
> Compar'd with these, Italian trills are tame.'

Still today such melodies fill sanctuaries around Scotland Sunday by Sunday, and also form the basis of General Assembly worship. Visitors from around the world, when asked what they enjoyed in particular about the General Assembly, invariably make reference to the unaccompanied psalm singing with which each day's business begins.

In the latter part of the eighteenth century a collection of Scriptural paraphrases appeared and these were accepted as a supplement to the psalter, the critical point being that they were still paraphrases of Holy Scripture. It would be another century before the established Church was ready for humanly inspired and composed hymns, though the progressive Relief Church did publish a hymn book as early as 1792. During the second half of the nineteenth century organs, choirs and anthems also made their debut and in 1898 the first edition of the *Church Hymnary* appeared, a joint venture of the Established, Free and United Presbyterian Churches. In 1927 the *Revised Church Hymnary* was introduced and continues in popular use to this day in a number of congregations. However, it was largely superseded by the *Church Hymnary* 3rd edn (*CH3*) of 1973, with a fourth edition due for publication in 2004.

My own generation grew up with the *Revised Church Hymnary*. While this did incorporate some metrical psalms and paraphrases, the general principle was to maintain the Psalter as a separate entity. In worship psalm portions were clearly announced and identified as such, the tune also being intimated by name and number. Many popular Victorian hymns survived the revision process, and in Sunday School we looked 'upward every day, sunshine on our faces'; we reflected on the question, 'O what can little hands do to please the King of Heaven?'; and we even looked forward to a time when 'with happy children, robed in snowy white' we would see our Saviour 'in that world so bright'. By contrast the 'new' hymn book, as *CH3* soon became known in the 1970s, struck a more contemporary note with hymns about 'shop-windows and playgrounds and swings in the park' and the God 'who mad'st the atom's hidden forces'. It also included a selection of the more popular psalm portions, scattered among the hymns according to theme, whereas in the past all 150 psalms and 67 paraphrases had been published, at the front of the hymn book, in their metrical entirety. Some feared this new policy would undermine the distinctiveness of the psalms, arguing, for example, that 'How lovely is thy dwelling place' should be announced as Psalm 84, not Hymn 4! Subsequently an edition was produced, with psalms and paraphrases at the front – just like the old days! Another innovation was the publication of an edition with the melody line of the tunes, though 'sol-fa' was dropped. *CH3* aimed high musically, with special commissions by contemporary Scottish composers such as Kenneth Leighton, Thomas Wilson, Martin Dalby, Frederick Rimmer, Reginald Barrett-Ayres and John Currie. It has to be said, however, that not many of these found their way into the typical congregation's core repertoire.

In fact, many congregations found *CH3* inadequate for their needs, with the result that a typical Sunday service would include a mix of traditional items from the hymn book and newer material quarried from a whole range of Christian song books which were appearing. For example, in the 1950s the 20th Century Church Light Music Group associated with names such as Geoffrey Beaumont and Patrick Appleford produced new, upbeat tunes for traditional hymns. The tune 'Camberwell' for the hymn 'At the name of Jesus' is about the only survivor of this particular genre. In the 1960s significant creative work was done by the Dunblane Music Group, officially called The Scottish Churches Music Consultation. Enduring names from this initiative include Erik Routley, Ian Fraser, Sydney Carter and Brian Wren and the group's publications *Dunblane Praises* and *New Songs of the Church* sold well. Such hymns and songs reflected contemporary themes, such as the environment, industrial society and modern city life. Ian Fraser's 'Lord Bring the Day to Pass' (*Songs of God's People*, No. 69) is a good example, with the bonus of giving continued life to Martin Shaw's tune 'Little Cornard' which disappeared when the hymn 'Hills of the north rejoice' failed to make it into *CH3*. The music of the Taizé community in France and the Iona Community nearer home also found their way into the worship of many congregations and, in due course, the Church itself produced its own supplements to the 'official' hymn book with *Songs for the Seventies* (1972), *Hymns for a Day* (1982) and *Songs of God's People* (1988). The last mentioned has been the most enduring and is an eclectic compilation of things old and new. Old favourites such as 'What a friend we have in Jesus' and 'I need thee every hour' were 'recovered', their exclusion from the *Church Hymnary* having occasioned much regret, if not outrage.

In the Preface to *Songs of God's People* John Bell, the convener of the compilation committee, observed that the book was 'a tribute to the diversity of the church, not just in its history and traditions, but also in the preferences of people within a single denomination'. It should be no surprise, he suggested, that people should vary in musical taste as in dress sense. Publications such as *Mission Praise* and the verses of writers such as Graham Kendrick, with hymns like 'Seek ye first the kingdom of God' and 'Shine, Jesus Shine', have also become firmly established.

In 1998 *Songs of God's People* was followed by *Common Ground*. This was thoroughly ecumenical, being compiled by a group representing seven Scottish churches, including the Roman Catholic Church, and it consolidated some of the more popular hymns from *Songs of God's People* such as 'Lord for the years' and 'We lay our broken world'. *Common Ground* also reflected John Bell's own distinctive adaptation of Scottish folk melodies to express words of prayer and praise. Tunes like the 'Mallaig Sprinkling Song', 'Bays of Harris' and 'The Iona Boat Song' are all used to good effect, following the example of Luther who took the popular folk tunes of his day and matched them to the sacred texts. The result is that today even more congregations, possibly even a majority, cull their Sunday praise from a variety of sources. Some have their own supplements. Others produce a weekly order of service sheet, with the words of non-hymnbook songs printed out under copyright licence. Musical accompaniment also goes beyond the traditional organ with praise bands comprising guitars, keyboard and drums. *CH4* when it appears will have to work hard to overcome the competition which has become so well established in so many places. The editorial policy to produce a comprehensive book has certainly been wise and many congregations will, no doubt, appreciate the convenience of having a wide diversity of choice in just the one publication.[3]

WORD AND SACRAMENT

At the heart of Christian worship there is a critical relationship between pulpit and table. Ministers are ordained to a ministry of word and sacrament, and both aspects have their place at the heart of Christian worship. One immediately apparent difference between the Church of Scotland and, say, the Roman Catholic Church is that in the latter church Mass is celebrated every Sunday, with an obligation upon the faithful to partake, whereas in the Kirk Communion is celebrated less frequently – perhaps quarterly or even half yearly. Certainly, this pattern varies and weekly Communion is available within the Church of Scotland, for example, in Edinburgh's St Giles' Cathedral and in Paisley Abbey. In recent years many congregations, while stopping short of weekly Communion, have moved to more frequent and less formal celebrations, perhaps monthly and on special occasions such as Christmas, Maundy Thursday and Easter.

Calvin favoured the celebration of the sacrament every Lord's Day. However, Knox's *First Book of Discipline* of 1561 considered that four times a year was sufficient frequency and this formed the basis for reformed church practice in Scotland. Knox's concern was 'that the superstition of the times may be avoided so far as may be'.[4] It has to be kept in mind that the great driving force behind the whole Reformation movement was the need to inform and educate ordinary Christian believers, so that they might read the Bible for themselves and be enabled to break free from superstitions surrounding religious rituals. It was, therefore, entirely to be expected that the Scottish Reformers should require intending communicants to be able to recite the Lord's Prayer, the Creed and the Ten Commandments before being admitted to the sacrament. This tradition of catechising the people before Communion continued well into the eighteenth century and the elder's pre-Communion visit today is a legacy of it, though today's visit is more likely to focus on pastoral interest than on theological or moral enquiry.

Closely related to the desire to create Christian understanding was the reformed emphasis on the preaching of the Word. From the Reformation up to the present day the sermon has been the centre piece of Kirk worship. Indeed, there was a time when the earlier part of the service was referred to simply as 'the preliminaries'. In Reformation times these would consist of prayer, reading of Scripture and the unaccompanied singing of psalms. The sermon would be substantial – lasting an hour or more – and its preparation would take up a significant proportion of the minister's week. Prayers would be extempore and, consequently, largely repetitive and it would not be expected that the sermon be read either. At the same time it was not expected that a minister should change his text too often, lest some of its saving truth be omitted. In the eighteenth century it was not unknown for a single verse of Scripture to engage the ministerial attention for up to a year. And, on the subject of reading or not reading the sermon, the famous Dr Archibald Charteris recorded that one Sunday in St Quivox Church, Ayr, where he was assistant minister, he entered the pulpit to discover that his sermon notes were upside down. Not daring to turn them round so publicly, he preached without them and did not rely on notes again until his old age. This was in 1858, indicating that at least by then the use of notes was becoming accepted, if not always acceptable.[5]

By this time there was a general move towards reforming worship and bringing both order and variety into it. In 1857, the year before Archibald Charteris found his sermon notes upside down in his pulpit, the Reverend Marshall Lang, a young Aberdeen minister, was censured by his presbytery for asking his members to stand to sing and sit to pray – the opposite of the practice of the times. The same year the Reverend Robert Lee, minister of Greyfriars Kirk in Edinburgh, also invited his congregation to stand for praise items, encouraged his members to kneel for prayer and introduced spoken congregational responses. For this he, too, was censured by his presbytery. He appealed to the General Assembly of 1859 which simply instructed him not to read prayers from a book. However, Lee persevered with his innovations, causing more controversy a few years later by the introduction of a harmonium and, subsequently, an organ.[6] Such innovations were becoming increasingly acceptable, however, and in 1867 the recently formed Church Service Society published a *Book of Common Order* (known also as *Euchologion*). This provided orders of service for Sunday worship, the administration of the sacraments and for marriages and funerals. Such services were not by any means prescribed, but their gradual adoption by ministers must have represented a great improvement on the endless recycling of the same old pious phrases which passed for extempore prayer.

More recent books of *Common Order* have been published officially from within the Church, though still 'authorised', as distinct from prescribed. There is no mandatory 'prayer book' within the Church of Scotland and most ministers, in leading public prayer, will draw material from a variety of sources, including their own inspiration and literary skill. Extempore prayer also continues as a legitimate option. The 1940 *Book of Common Order,* prepared by the Assembly's Committee on Public Worship and Aids to Devotion, which acknowledged an indebtedness to its 1928 predecessor, held sway until a new edition appeared in 1979. That, however, proved to be too long a gap, with the result that by then many ministers had already moved beyond the very traditional 'thee/thou' language of the 1940 book and were drawing on the great variety of liturgical resources available. This had the very positive advantage of broadening and deepening the spirituality of congregations. The 1979 book provided services in both traditional and contemporary forms, but it did not achieve the popularity of its predecessor and became, indeed, the focus of an interesting and illuminating controversy.

The 1940 book opened with full services, including prayers, for morning and evening worship, eleven in all, then went on to offer services for Baptism and Holy Communion, marriage, funerals, ordination of elders, dedication of memorials and prayers for the seasons of the Christian year. The 1979 book, by contrast, began with three full services for Holy Communion, followed by an outline for 'the main Sunday Service when the Lord's Supper is not celebrated'.[7] Full services for such occasions were promised in a companion volume which would follow. In adopting this approach the Committee on Public Worship and Aids to Devotion was making a liturgical point, namely, that Eucharistic worship is the weekly norm. Writing in the Introduction to the book the Convener, Dr Stewart Todd, explained: 'By this arrangement the Committee gives clear expression again to the normative character of the service of word and sacrament, which character was undoubtedly recognised by the Reformers, as it has been down the centuries by the

Universal Church.' The Introduction acknowledged that 'to describe the Sunday morning worship of most churches in Scotland negatively as "Morning Service where Holy Communion is not celebrated" is perhaps unfortunate' and went on to affirm in positive terms 'the rich experience of the Holy Spirit' which came from the hearing and preaching of the Word in Church of Scotland worship. Nevertheless the Committee held to the view that, even when the sacrament was not celebrated the eucharistic order of worship should be followed.[8] The Committee's position was entirely tenable, but it did not play particularly well with some within the Church and in 1987 the General Assembly accepted a motion instructing the Panel on Worship (as the Committee had now become) 'without delay to proceed with the production of a new *Book of Common Order*'. In the debate on the motion it was made very clear to the Panel that the model of any new book should be 1940 and not 1979. The Panel duly obeyed and obliged and the 1994 edition appeared, was well received and continues to be well used, reflecting as it does the best in traditional and contemporary liturgical material.

CHILDREN, COMMUNION AND CHURCH MEMBERSHIP

One of the most significant debates affecting the life and worship of the Church of Scotland in recent years has centred on the question of the inclusion of baptised children in the celebration of the Lord's Supper. The debate began in the early 1970s and touched on questions of theology, worship, nurture, practice and procedure and the rules governing church membership. It will be helpful now to use that debate as a lens through which to view changing patterns of congregational life, church membership and worship over recent decades.

A typical mid- to late-twentieth-century Sunday worship pattern within the Church of Scotland involved children attending the first part of the service, during which the minister would address some words particularly to them, before they departed to the church hall for Sunday School. From time to time 'family services' might be held, which involved all-age worship. Such services would typically be linked to occasions such as Guide 'Thinking Day', Mothering Sunday and the great Christian festivals. On the quarterly or half-yearly Sundays when Communion was celebrated with a fair degree of formality the children would probably not join in the congregational worship at all. It was this pattern which came increasingly to be questioned as part of a whole reassessment of the nurture and place of children within the life of the Church.

As already noted, much emphasis has been placed on the centrality of the sermon in reformed worship. The design of many churches, with high central pulpit, underlines the point, and the message which inevitably comes across is that Sunday worship is an adult activity. Silence and concentration become basic requirements for listening to a serious sermon, perhaps lasting anything up to half an hour, and the presence of lively children will certainly not be conducive to creating such an atmosphere. Better then, it was argued, that the children receive their Christian education in an environment more fitted to their needs in Sunday School. Where congregations followed all-age worship and learning programmes, the same Bible readings and themes could be explored by the different age groups and the creative minister would be able to introduce these in the opening part of the service where all were assembled together.

Just as the Church of Scotland has fostered a serious approach to preaching, so it has encouraged a solemn approach to Holy Communion, also referred to as the Lord's Supper. We have noted that the Reformers' preference for quarterly observance was a reaction to superstitions surrounding the medieval Mass and, certainly, a corollary of a less frequent partaking is the creation of a sense of occasion, combined with opportunity for due preparation. Again, we have noted the *First Book of Discipline*'s requirement that intending communicants should be able to recite the Lord's Prayer, the Ten Commandments and the Creed, and this further evolved into the practice of regular catechising by minister or elder prior to each celebration of the Sacrament. Also, included in the pre-Communion examination would be issues of personal life and behaviour. The message that came across, therefore, was that spiritual knowledge and moral worthiness were pre-conditions of participation. Taken together, it is hardly surprising that what emerged was a culture which deterred people from coming to the Lord's Table, lest they should 'eat and drink unworthily' and so bring damnation upon themselves. Indeed, a regular feature of the eighteenth-century Communion service was 'the fencing of the table'. This consisted of supplementary sermons, delivered immediately prior to the reception of the elements, warning of the risks of unworthy participation, and the handing in of a token signifying worthiness to partake. Still, in much of the Highlands and Islands to this day, many choose to remain as adherents rather than become communicant members of the Church.

Today the Church no longer requires instruction and examination prior to each celebration of Communion. The elder's visit, as we have already observed, is more of a pastoral and social call, expressing the church's interest in the life of the individual and family and encouraging their involvement within the life of the church. The focus now has shifted to preparation for admission to the Lord's Table for the first time, a process usually comprising a series of classes led by the minister, traditionally known as 'First Communicants' Classes', but also referred to as 'Church Membership Classes' or some other such title. At the conclusion of these classes, typically involving around six weekly meetings, a special service is held at which those who have completed the course make public profession of their faith and are formally admitted to the Lord's Table. The Admission itself is an act of the Kirk Session and representatives of the Kirk Session join with the minister in the ceremony which includes the traditional right hand of fellowship. On a personal note, I recall a particularly moving moment in my ministry when, for the first time, I welcomed as a new communicant member someone whom I had baptised as an infant.

It was practices and procedures such as these which were challenged in a series of debates in the Church during the last quarter of the twentieth century. In 1972 the General Assembly appointed a Special Committee anent Church Membership and part of the remit given to the Committee was 'to examine the theological significance of confessing the faith for church membership'. Underlying this was the theological question of the relationship between the sacraments and membership of the Church. The Church of Scotland recognises the two sacraments of Baptism and Holy Communion. Baptism has traditionally been understood as the sacrament of initiation into the Church. There is a long-standing debate over infant *versus* believer's baptism and some churches, most notably the Baptist Church, withhold baptism until the individual is able to make his or her own profession of faith. Upon doing so the person is then admitted to all the privileges and rights of Church membership, including the Sacrament of Holy Communion. Meanwhile, at the other end of the spectrum, the Orthodox Churches of the east also baptise infants but, in doing so, receive the children fully into the life of the Church, so that when they are of an age physically to cope with the mechanics, they share in Communion with their parents and the congregation.

There is a certain logic in these positions, in that both recognise Baptism as the sacrament of initiation which leads naturally to the privileges of Church membership, including the fellowship of the Lord's Table. By contrast, there is an arguable lack of logic in those churches which permit infants to be received into the membership of the Church through Baptism, but then require some further hurdle to be cleared before admission to the Lord's Table. On the other hand, there were undeniably strong historical and educational arguments in favour of the Church's traditional practice. It allowed for the child to be baptised and welcomed into the Church, while at the same time looking to parents and to the Church itself to make a commitment to the Christian nurture of the child. The fruit of that commitment came when 'years of discretion' were reached and the child, now a young adult, could, of his or her own volition, make a personal and public profession of faith and be received into the full communicant membership of the Church. Many would say, 'What is wrong with that?'

The practical answer was that the system just wasn't working. In the late 1950s and early 1960s some 50,000 infants a year were being baptised into the Church of Scotland. By the late 1970s and early 1980s, the point at which these individuals ought to have been coming through the system into the Church's communicant membership, the number of professions of faith was around 14,000 annually – less than a third. Where were the others? Many sociological factors were reflected in these statistics, and now we fully recognise the postmodern phenomenon of reluctance to make commitments in a whole range of directions. Nevertheless, there were real questions for the Church in face of such a striking failure of its Christian nurture policy.

The theological answer to the question, 'what was wrong with the policy', was that it perpetuated the notion of Communion as a prize for those who passed the intellectual and moral tests, and did not take sufficiently seriously its sacramental nature as a means of grace. The question now being raised was whether inclusion within the sacramental family should be recognised as a vital means of nurturing the child towards a personal profession of faith, rather than as something which should be delayed until such a profession had been made. Indeed, what kind of statement was the Church making in excluding children from so much of its routine worship and especially from such a central act of worship as Holy Communion?

Issues such as these came to the fore in a report to the General Assembly of 1982 from a Working Group on 'The Lord's Supper and the Children of the Church'.[9] I had the task of convening this Group, which drew together representatives of the Panel on Doctrine, the Panel on Worship, the Youth Education Committee and the Board of Practice and Procedure. In our study we drew on the earlier work of the Committee anent Church Membership and also on a 1977 report by the Parish Education Committee which had stressed the nurturing capacity of the sacrament as a means of grace and concluded that there appeared to be no good doctrinal reason for debarring children from Holy Communion. The 1982 report, having reviewed the theological, pastoral and educational issues involved, came to the same conclusion. We noted that, strictly speaking, there was no church law preventing children receiving communion under present arrangements, provided they were able to make an appropriate and adequate profession of faith. However, what we sought was not a mere refinement of existing procedures but a whole new approach which emphasised the nurturing links between the two sacraments.

Our report noted that profession of faith (sometimes also referred to as 'confirmation') admitted the person not only to Communion but also to such rights and responsibilities of Church membership as eligibility for election to office within the church, for example, the eldership, and election to serve on a vacancy committee. The effect of this was almost to make admission to Communion a rite of initiation into church membership, when, theologically, that was really the function of Baptism. Why, we wondered, did admission to Communion have to be connected to admission to administrative membership? Rather, we argued, let admission to the Lord's Table flow naturally from Baptism. Meantime, by all means, retain a place for public profession of faith as a rite of passage into the practical responsibilities of mature church membership. Such an approach would allow an appropriate distinction to be made between grace and law and also enable the development of a logical sequence of belonging. Baptism would declare that the child belonged to the Church; the nurture of the child within the full life and worship of the Church, including the sacrament, could contribute to the growing child's growing sense of belonging; and, finally, profession of faith would allow the young adult to own personally that he or she belonged and was ready now to take their share of responsibility within the life of the Church.

Our 1982 report also attempted to address some practical issues. What was envisaged was that, in practice, children from about the age of seven could begin receiving Communion with their parents and, bearing in mind issues of dignity and decorum, there was also a clear recognition that the children should be of an age 'to sit through the service without unduly disturbing the good order of worship'. The report further made clear that there was no question of indiscriminate giving of the sacrament to infants, or 'marching in a Sunday School'. Given the 'black-tie' solemnity that characterised many Communion services the reality of the situation was that the Group was effectively thinking of children, initially at least, sharing in the less formal Communion celebrations already referred to such as at Christmas and Easter. As a measure of the gulf to be bridged I recall a colleague telling me of his proposal to introduce an informal celebration of the Sacrament, following the Easter Family Service. This was greeted by the comment from a senior elder, 'but Easter's a happy time'. The risen Christ may have been known to his followers at Emmaus in the breaking of bread, but there would be none of that in that parish!

Looking back twenty years on that report and the work which went into it, I am reminded that our hope was that, by including children in the Sacrament, the Church would come to a greater appreciation of what it meant to be the family of God, gathered round the Lord's Table. To us it seemed that banishing the children at such a time was equivalent to excluding them from Christmas dinner, something most families would find unthinkable. I also recall making the point, when introducing the report in the General Assembly, that ministers cast around (often with increasing desperation as Sunday draws ever closer) for visual aids to illustrate the children's address, yet when we take those most powerful visual aids of bread and wine the children are not there.

The General Assembly of 1982 was persuaded that this was a good proposal and supported the recommendation that enabling legislation should be introduced. This would have allowed baptised children to be admitted to Communion, provided the Kirk Session was satisfied that they could respond, appropriately, to the general requirement that the Lord's Table was open to any baptised person who loved the Lord and responded in faith to the invitation, 'Take, eat'. Recognising that this was a major departure from traditional practice the Assembly resolved that Barrier Act procedure was required. When the views of presbyteries came into the Principal Clerk at the end of the year it was apparent that the consent of a majority of presbyteries had not been given. Twenty were in favour, twenty-eight against and, accordingly, the General Assembly of 1983 had no choice but to depart from the matter.

However, the question did not go away and in 1989 it was raised again from the floor of the General Assembly and a remit given to the new Board of Parish Education. A fresh working group was established under the convenership of Professor Robert Davidson. A report, making broadly similar recommendations to that of its predecessor of ten years earlier, was approved by the General Assembly of 1991. This time the Barrier Act was cleared with thirty presbyteries now in favour and only eighteen against, and the General Assembly of 1992 passed the required legislation. This means that the position in the Church of Scotland today is that, provided a Kirk Session is satisfied that baptised children 'are being nurtured within the life and worship of the Church and love the Lord and respond in faith to the invitation, "take, eat"', it may admit such children to the Lord's Table.[10] The legislation further requires that the names of such children are not to be added to the Communion Roll of the congregation until they have made public profession of faith. While this sounds somewhat anomalous, it merely reflects the fact that the Communion Roll comprises a list of names of those who have the legal and administrative rights of congregational membership as well as the privilege of partaking in the Lord's Supper. Perhaps terms such as 'Congregational Roll' or 'Membership Roll' would be preferable, though doubtless the question would then arise as to whether children were members of the congregation or not! This point was addressed to the extent that in 1995 the Board of Practice and Procedure recommended that congregational rolls maintain lists of names of all associated with the life of the congregation, annotated so as to identify communicants who have made a profession of faith, children who have been admitted to Communion prior to profession of faith and adult adherents who worship regularly but have not sought formal membership of the church.[11]

In a culture of inclusiveness there is inevitably administrative untidiness. The book of Proverbs reminds us that 'where no oxen are, the crib is clean'[12] and people, too, bringing the often untidy realities of their own situations, find their own comfort levels within the life of the Church. In both my parish ministries I had a body of regular worshippers who did not wish to make the commitment implied by public profession of faith and so have their names placed on the Communion Roll of the congregation. I was anxious lest, on a Communion Sunday, such people should feel excluded because, not being on the roll, they received no Communion card and might therefore feel embarrassed on turning up to find people handing in cards of invitation, when they had none. To direct them to the gallery, as spectators, would be grossly discourteous; to ask them to stay away unthinkable. The solution was to dispense with

Communion cards altogether, to include such regularly worshipping adherents within the elders' districts and, on a Communion Sunday, to leave it as a matter of their choice and conscience as to whether they received or simply passed the elements.

Similar concerns over pastoral untidiness were expressed by the Board of Parish Education in its 1995 report when it raised the question of unbaptised children growing up within the life and worship of the Church and argued for the recently passed legislation to be amended to provide for them also to have a place at the Lord's Table. This was remitted to the Panel on Doctrine which the following year recommended that, while ministers should be sensitive to particular pastoral situations, there should be no change to the general rule that Baptism should be administered prior to participation in the Lord's Supper. In a situation where someone was communicating, not having been baptised, pastoral steps should be taken towards the Baptism of that person.

During 1996 the Board of Parish Education conducted a survey of Kirk Sessions as to how the new legislation was working. The Board's report to the Assembly of 1997 expressed disappointment that only 942 out of 1597 (59 per cent) Kirk Sessions responded, but these responses showed that, of the 942, 514 had resolved to admit children, 205 had refused, 129 were still considering the matter and 95 had not discussed the matter.[13] On the basis that those who embraced the change would be more likely to say so than those who had not, this suggests that around one-third of congregations were implementing the new procedures. A question seeking to ascertain the numbers of children now receiving Communion in terms of the 1992 legislation has recently been included in the annual statistical return compiled by the Board of Practice and Procedure but, at time of writing, data is not available. My own sense is that the numbers are not large and, personally, I find this disappointing. It remains my view that the Sacrament is the family meal of the people of God, both in its solemn remembering of the night in which the Lord was betrayed and in its joyful eucharistic meeting with the risen Christ. By resolving to break the link between admission to the Sacrament and admission to the obligations of church membership, and by no longer measuring minimal church commitment as attendance at Communion once in three years,[14] the Church has sought to liberate the Sacrament from the realm of law and acknowledge its place firmly within the sphere of grace. At the same time, more frequent, less formal celebrations have led to a new understanding of the Sacrament within the regular life of the worshipping community and this has contributed much to the renewal and refreshment, not just of worship, but of the whole life of the Church.

NOTES

1 Millar Patrick, *Four Centuries of Scottish Psalmody*, London: Oxford University Press, 1949, p. 133.

2 See Finlay Macdonald, in T. M. Devine and P. Logue (eds), *Being Scottish*, Edinburgh: Polygon at Edinburgh, 2002, pp. 159–61.

3 I am indebted to the Reverend Douglas Galbraith, Secretary to the Panels on Doctrine and Worship, for some of the detail in this and the preceding paragraph.

4 *First Book of Discipline*, The Ninth Head concerning the Policie of the Kirk.

5 I am grateful to Mrs Alison Twaddle, General Secretary of the Church of Scotland Guild, for this anecdote which she used in her 2003 Charteris Lecture.

6 See J. H. S. Burleigh, *A Church History of Scotland*, London: Oxford University Press, 1960, p. 388.

7 *Book of Common Order*, 1979, p. 42.

8 *Book of Common Order*, 1979, Introduction.

9 See Assembly Reports, 1982, pp. 467–77.

10 The provision is now incorporated in Act V, 2000, section 15.

11 Reports to the General Assembly, 1995, p. 3.

12 Proverbs 14:4.

13 Assembly Reports, 1997, p. 25/13.

14 Act VI, 1938 allowed the Kirk Session to remove from the Communion Roll the names of those 'who by abstention from Communion for a period of three years, without a reason satisfactory to the Kirk Session, manifest their indifference'. Now a more general test is applied, namely, has the person 'shown sufficient interest or taken an adequate share in the worship, mission and service of the Church'? (Act VI, 2000, s. 9).

6

Change and the Church's Ministry

MINISTER AND PARISH

The parish ministry has long been regarded as one of the great strengths of the Church of Scotland. It is important to emphasise the word 'parish'. The Declaratory Articles speak of the Church's commitment to 'bring the ordinances of religion to the people in every parish of Scotland through a territorial ministry'[1] and J. T. Cox asserts: 'a minister should not refuse to perform ministerial functions for a person resident in his [sic] parish without sufficient reason'.[2] The principle enshrined here is an ancient one and it expresses the commitment of the Church, not just to its own members, but to all who seek the grace and comfort of the Gospel. In the nineteenth century both the Established Church and Free Church held to the principle of an establishment of religion, by which was meant the duty of the State to ensure that the religious needs of the nation were met by an established church, though other churches were free to exist as well. At the 1843 Disruption the Free Church had walked away from what it saw as a corrupt establishment, but Chalmers' intention had been to return to a pure establishment which would respect the Church's spiritual independence. By contrast, the United Presbyterian Church took a completely different view and adopted the principle of 'voluntarism'. This held, quite simply, that those who wanted a church should be prepared to meet the costs involved. Unchecked, this road led to an entrepreneurial philosophy. Just as today a supermarket chain would undertake consumer research to determine the optimum location for a new store, so the Church would look for its own market niche and supportive client base.

Indeed, I recall, in the early years of my ministry, an elder declining to take part in a parish visitation on the grounds that, having grown up in the United Presbyterian tradition, he didn't agree with the parish principle. The Established Church certainly did, and the 1929 reunion, which brought all three strands of nineteenth-century Presbyterianism together, found the solution in a church which was funded by the voluntary giving of its members, but was, at the same time, committed to maintaining a church and ministerial presence in those areas, where to do so was not economically viable. The Christian principle of the strong supporting the weak underlined this approach. Better-off congregations were to pay their way and contribute to a central fund which supported the ministry in remote, sparsely populated islands and in areas of urban deprivation. Despite declining membership and financial pressures the Church of Scotland remains as committed as ever to this principle.

It is important to stress this point. The 2001 census indicated that over two million Scots, around 40 per cent of the population, claimed a connection with the Church of Scotland. This number vastly exceeds the number of names on Communion Rolls which is around 600,000. Even this statistic includes many whose membership is nominal. How much more tenuous and sentimental is the connection of the great majority of the two million? And yet, the fact that it is there at all reflects the parish-based culture of a national church, with an interest and a concern for the whole community. Cox's statement that a minister should not lightly refuse the ordinances of religion to those outwith the membership of the congregation is a reminder that ministry is not just to the congregation but to the parish. We must weigh very carefully the effect upon the Church's witness of turning people away on the grounds that they have hitherto shown little interest in the Church. Shall we also turn them away on Christmas Eve? Of course the Church must have standards and expectations, but if we make it apparent that the minister's role is to minister exclusively to the active and committed membership of the Church then we sever a vital evangelical and pastoral link with the people of Scotland.

WOMEN IN MINISTRY

In 1931, just two years after the union, the Marchioness of Aberdeen brought before the General Assembly a petition, bearing 338 signatures, which sought the ordination of women to the ministry, eldership and the diaconate.[3] The petition maintained that 'the continued exclusion of women from these offices is contrary to the mind and teaching of Christ and that it limits the operation of the Spirit of God'. It further declared the petitioners' conviction 'that women no less than men are called to the ministry of the Church and that the Church is poorer by reason of women being debarred from the ministry as well as the other offices'.[4] The following year the Woman's Guild brought a separate petition asking that a number of women be given places as corresponding (speaking, but not voting) members of the General Assembly. Meanwhile, yet another petition that year, from the Marchioness of Ailsa, urged that, rather than pursuing the question of admission to the ministry and eldership, the Church should seek to develop existing opportunities for women. The intriguingly named Committee on the Place of Women in the Church, to which these various petitions were remitted, came back in 1933 with a recommendation that women should be ordained to the diaconate and the eldership, but not the ministry. The Committee also recommended that the corresponding member proposal should be approved, as a temporary measure, pending the decision on women and the eldership. However, after the proposals were referred to presbyteries, the only change agreed was that women be admitted to the diaconate.

The question arose again in 1957, when Overtures on the question of women in the eldership were presented to the General Assembly by the presbyteries of Aberdeen, Ayr and Kirkcaldy. These were taken together and the Assembly decided to remit the matters raised in them to presbyteries for consideration. The following year, in response to the comments of presbyteries, the Assembly appointed another Committee on the Place of Women in the Church. (Evidently, despite constituting a majority of the membership they still didn't know their place!) The remit of the Committee was to examine more closely the returns from Presbyteries; to consult with persons and bodies, statutory and otherwise, interested in the service of women to the Church; to consider the whole question of the co-operation of men and women in the Church: and report to the next General Assembly.

In its report to the 1959 Assembly the Committee gave an indication of varied feeling and divided opinion. The views of the five largest presbyteries on the 1957 overtures were noted – Edinburgh in favour of women elders by 113 votes to 103, Glasgow in favour by 178 votes to 74, Aberdeen in favour unanimously, Dundee against unanimously and Hamilton against by a majority (unspecified). The Moderator of the Presbytery of Deer gave his casting vote in favour, and the Presbytery of Islay, while supportive, expressed a concern that women, being more likely to attend meetings, might 'come to hold the dominant voice in the Church'. The Presbytery of Bathgate had no theological or practical objection, but noted 'that there is strong adverse prejudice, not least among the women of the Church'. As well as reporting in such terms, the Committee offered a considered analysis of the issues from the perspectives of Scripture, tradition, church history and ecumenism and its report was referred again to presbyteries and also to the Central Committee of the Woman's Guild and the Order of Deaconesses.[5]

The following year, 1960, the Committee reported that twenty-seven presbyteries were definitely in favour of women being eligible for the eldership, fourteen were against, with twenty-three undecided. Of those which expressed a view, eighteen wished to see women admitted to the ministry with twenty-one against. Encouraged by the positive opinion expressed on women elders the Committee, as its final act before being discharged, brought an Overture incorporating enabling legislation to be sent down under the Barrier Act. The following year the Committee on Classifying Returns to Overtures reported a 'dead heat', with thirty-four presbyteries For and thirty-four Against. Not receiving the support of a majority of presbyteries, the measure fell.

However, the issue was certainly not going away and in 1963 Miss Mary Lusk, BD (after her marriage, the Reverend Mary Levison), presented a petition to the General Assembly asking that it 'take the necessary action to enable the appropriate Presbytery to proceed with the ordination of the Petitioner'.[6] Miss Lusk had been commissioned as a deaconess in 1954 and three years later licensed as a preacher by the Presbytery of Dalkeith. At the time of her petition she was Assistant Chaplain to the University of Edinburgh and 'believed herself called of God to the Ministry of Word and Sacraments'. After the petition was received and heard there were three motions before the General Assembly – a proposal to grant the crave, a proposal to reject the crave and a proposal to remit the petition to the recently formed Panel on Doctrine, the body which had inherited the remit of the previous Special Committee on the Place of Women in the Church. It was this third proposal which carried, and those in favour of change could take comfort from the fact that the motion which attracted least support was the one urging a straightforward rejection of the petition. The following year the Panel reserved its position as far as women in the ministry was concerned, but came out clearly in favour of women elders. The report was sent to presbyteries and in 1965 the Panel advised the Assembly that presbyteries which had responded indicated support for opening the eldership to women by thirty-one presbyteries to eleven, and for admitting women to the ministry by nineteen votes to eighteen. Clearly opinion was shifting and this time the Overture promoting legislation which would enable women to become elders was successful. The General Assembly of 1966, having learned that forty-five presbyteries had voted in favour, with seventeen against, proceeded to convert the Overture into a standing law of the Church.

In 1967 the Panel brought a further report on the question of the ordination of women to the ministry, with the proposal that this be received as fulfilling the remit given to it in 1960 and 'be sent to Presbyteries for their information'. The Panel Convener, the Reverend Dr John Heron, in presenting the report, stated that the Panel was 'not of one mind on the matter', but had, in any event, seen its task, not as making a definite recommendation, but rather one of 'bringing into the open the theological principles involved in a particular matter to guide the thinking of the Courts of the Church, which alone have the right to make the final decisions'.[7] The Panel's neutral recommendation was in line with this approach, but an amendment from the floor proposed that the Principal Clerk and the Procurator 'be instructed to draft an Overture to be sent down under the Barrier Act enabling women to be ordained to the Ministry on the same terms and conditions as men'. This was carried by 397 votes to 298. The Overture, duly drafted and approved, was considered by presbyteries and the following year it was reported that it had received the approval of forty-five presbyteries, with seventeen disapproving and two tied. Accordingly in 1968 the General Assembly passed the historic legislation which enabled women to be ordained to the ministry.

The statistical reports of the Board of Practice and Procedure to the General Assembly of 2003 showed that, at 31 December 2002, of 1061 ministers serving in charges, 164 were women and 897 were men. This works out at slightly less than one in five and suggests that the anxieties of the Presbytery of Islay, referred to above, were unfounded. In terms of ministerial personnel women are far from a dominant voice. In the higher courts of the Church (Presbytery and General Assembly) they also continue to form a minority – a not insignificant minority, even in the General Assembly, but a minority nevertheless. Only at the local Kirk Session level do women approximate to or form a majority, though notwithstanding the strictures of the 1991 General Assembly, there are still some Kirk Sessions which remain all-male bastions.

That year the Board of Practice and Procedure brought a report to the General Assembly in which it expressed concern that, twenty-five years after the recognition of women's eligibility for the eldership, on the same terms and conditions as men, there were a number of ministers and Kirk Sessions which were treating the 1966 legislation as permissive. The Board acknowledged that 'the fact that a Kirk Session has always chosen men from the total number of those eligible is not itself a breach of the law', but went on to declare quite clearly that, 'if, as a matter of policy or principle a Kirk Session has deliberately restricted its choice to men, and thus denied the eligibility of women, the law has been contravened'.[8] The General Assembly endorsed this view and reiterated a 1986 invitation to presbyteries to consult with those Kirk Sessions which as yet had no women elders, with a view to urging them to consider appointing women to the eldership. Such Kirk Sessions, it should be said, are now a minority. In the great majority of congregations women and men work happily and creatively together in the service of congregation and parish.

Women in ministry are also a well-established reality in the life of the Church although they remain a minority and some prejudice still endures. Given that women are eligible on the same terms and conditions as men, it would be contrary to the law of the Church for a Nominating (Vacancy) Committee to take a decision in principle that only male ministers would be considered for a vacancy. In practice, however, the expectation of many congregations, which have not been served by a woman minister, is that the minister will be a man. Tellingly, where congregations have had a woman minister they often go for the same again! Nevertheless, while many women have had happy and successful ministries, they have also had to cope with a subtle but powerful pressure to prove themselves. There is more than a touch of condescension in remarks like, 'I've never seen a woman conduct a wedding; you did it very nicely'. We are now quite accustomed to women bus drivers and airline pilots. I wonder if they receive similar comments from passengers!

In 1995 the General Assembly established a 'Gender Attitude Project' and one of the issues the Project Group noted in its first report was the need for 'Church members to examine gender attitudes and issues as they affect their own lives and structures, not least in the selection of ministers at time of vacancies'.[9] In 2001 the Project published a booklet entitled *The Stained Glass Ceiling* which, while acknowledging the changes in church law which affirmed the equality of men and women in the government of the Church, also pointed out that 'the law of the Church cannot change attitudes or encourage people to rethink their theology or the reasons why they hold certain views'.[10] Accordingly, the Project, in its final report, to the General Assembly of 2002, called for 'forms of education and awareness raising – not necessarily with the aim of everyone believing the same, but certainly with the aim of nurturing relationships of respect, mutuality and justice between all people within the Church'.[11]

The phrase 'Stained Glass Ceiling' was readily seized upon to express the view that there were levels within the Church beyond which women could not rise. In particular it was noted, within the Church and by the media, that a woman had never held the office of Moderator of the General Assembly. Certainly most convenerships of Assembly Boards and Committees have been held by women, namely, Social Responsibility, Church and Nation, Practice and Procedure, Ministry, Communication, Nomination, Assembly Council and World Mission, as have a number of senior administrative posts, including the principal clerkship of the General Assembly. Women have also served as presbytery moderators and clerks.

In early 2003 a letter from the Reverend Kathy Galloway, Leader of the Iona Community, and also signed by 139 church women, appeared in the press. It expressed profound regret that, 'in a church where women make up two-thirds of the membership and have for over thirty years been ordained as elders and ministers, thus becoming fully eligible for nomination and election as Moderator of the General Assembly, **not one woman** has been considered to be suitable or worthy to moderate the General assembly and to act for one year as our church's principal public representative'. The nomination of Dr Alison Elliot, a former Convener of the Church and Nation Committee, Convener of the Central Council of ACTS and Session Clerk of Edinburgh's Greyfriars Tolbooth and Highland Kirk, to be Moderator of the 2004 General Assembly, has finally made good this failure.

VOCATION AND PROFESSION

The ministry of word and sacrament has traditionally been regarded, not as a job, but as a calling or vocation. Thomas Chalmers subsequently repudiated a comment made during his early ministry at Kilmany in Fife, but it was certainly noteworthy. The twenty-five-year-old Chalmers declared: 'after the satisfactory discharge of his parish duties a minister may enjoy five days in the week of uninterrupted leisure, for the prosecution of any science in which his taste may dispose him to engage'.[12] That was in 1805 and two hundred years later the old joke about a one-day week still dies hard. Yet, while ultimately accountable to the presbytery, the reality was that ministers were largely solo operators who enjoyed an extraordinary degree of security of tenure. It was not until 1972 that the General Assembly introduced a retirement age of seventy for ministers, though ministers still in a charge to which they were inducted before that date can remain in post for as long as they feel able to discharge their responsibilities. In 1996 the age of retirement was further reduced to sixty-five. At the same time the principle of tenure has gradually been eroded with an increasing number of appointments made on the basis of reviewable tenure. This allows a presbytery to give a minister notice to quit when, for example, a vacancy occurs in a neighbouring parish, thereby providing the opportunity for a union of two vacant charges. The minister concerned is normally given six months' notice so that he or she can find another charge. My own view is that security of tenure and right of call are two sides of a coin, and that if the one is to be qualified so, reasonably, should the other. That is to say, there may be a case for establishing a process which enables a minister, whose tenure is called in by the presbytery, to be offered another charge, rather than having to apply for vacancies in the normal way. However, despite various reports over the years the issue of call and tenure is one circle which the Church finds very difficult to square. It may be that the Task Force for Change, due to report to the General Assembly of 2004, will have more success.

Today, while still affirming the ministry as a vocation, the Church also takes a professional approach. In its report to the General Assembly of 1987 the Maintenance of the Ministry Committee stated bluntly: 'The ministry is no different from any other profession.'[13] This was in the context of a report on pastoral support of ministers and within a section headed, somewhat ominously, 'Incompetence'. With great courage and honesty the Committee articulated its concern

> that the Church's efforts to support its ministry should be credible in the eyes of thinking members of the Church, and believes that for this to be so it must be made clear that there is a readiness in the Church and ministry to tackle the problem of ministers whose lack of capability appears to show that no amount of support, advice or other help will enable them to meet the demands of the ministry.[14]

To follow up its concerns the Committee even established a sub-committee, initially called the 'Incompetence Committee', but subsequently restyled, more positively, the 'Committee on Professional Standards and Conduct'. This Committee compared notes with industry, commerce and professions such as teaching and medicine and presented to the General Assembly of 1993 a document entitled 'Balance of Ministerial Duties'. At the same time it intimated its intention of bringing forward a 'Code of Professional Conduct' for ministers. Two years later, following consultation with the Assembly Council and the Board of Practice and Procedure this latter document appeared.

The 'Balance of Ministerial Duties' document described the basic tasks of an ordained minister. These included such obvious things as the conduct of public worship, pastoral care, weddings and funerals, Christian education and sharing in the work of the courts of the Church. The document concluded with the statement:

> To achieve a competent ministry and to pursue excellence in ministry, a minister ... needs to exercise sound stewardship of time and ability, to have good interpersonal skills, to co-operate with colleagues in the discharge of his/her duties, both in the every day tasks of ministry and to secure adequate cover for leisure and holidays, to have a sound devotional life and to find time for both study and training and for adequate leisure and recreation.[15]

The 'Professional Standards' document covered areas such as provision of absence cover, observance of confidentiality, propriety in pastoral relationships, not charging personal fees for baptisms, weddings and funerals, respect for the pastoral sphere of colleagues and 'circumspection in the receiving and disbursing of monies for church purposes'. The Maintenance of the Ministry Committee sought the Assembly's approval for what it called the Guidelines on Professional Standards and Conduct within the Church 'as a basis for ministerial development and support'. However, following debate, the Assembly chose to send these Guidelines back for further consideration and report the following year. When the matter came back in 1996 the Guidelines were offered 'for use in Education, Training and Development, recognising that ... in themselves [they] have no status in law, but that they do reflect the Committee's view of best practice in Ministry'. The Committee also expressed the view that the Guidelines would 'develop and evolve as time goes on'.[16] In receiving them the Assembly simply noted the Committee's intention to include them in the *Minister's Handbook* and encourage their use in the ways indicated.

It was clear that the Assembly was reluctant to go beyond the status of 'guidelines' and prescribe definitive regulation or law. The concern was that, if given such force, the matters enumerated could be held as exhaustive, and that conduct, self-evidently unprofessional, but not identified as such in the Guidelines, might then go unchallenged. The prevailing view was that it was certainly helpful to have a written code, but that sufficient sanctions were already available to presbyteries in terms of their general powers of supervision. If a minister offended in the areas of life or doctrine then procedures were in place to deal with that. Similarly, if a minister's conduct was such as to create an unsatisfactory state in a congregation, a situation which failed to respond to pastoral intervention by the presbytery, and which, in the presbytery's view, would continue so long as the minister remained in post, then there were procedures in place to deal with that as well. This was a moot point as far as the Committee on the Maintenance of the Ministry was concerned. It argued strongly in its 1993 report that the 'Unsatisfactory State' legislation, which operated on the basis of 'irretrievable breakdown' rather than 'the apportioning of blame', was not adequate to deal with straightforward incompetence. However, while the Guidelines make an important statement about a 'professional' ministry, the situation remains that the only ways of dissolving a pastoral tie between minister and congregation are the exercise of discipline on grounds of life or doctrine and the recognition of an irretrievable breakdown of the pastoral relationship.[17]

COLLABORATIVE, REFLECTIVE AND FORMATIVE MINISTRY

In 2000 the Board of Ministry presented a major report to the General Assembly entitled 'Ministers of the Gospel.' This was the outcome of a decision of the previous year's Assembly to accept a proposal from the Board that it should 'make an in-depth study of the theology and practice of ordained ministry, so that the Church of Scotland would have a clear statement of the thinking that directs the Board's work'.[18] The report drew on a consultative process within the Church, sociological analysis of trends in contemporary Scotland and the insights of other churches, in particular the Presbyterian Church (USA). Three varying, but inter-related perspectives helped shape the report in its aim of bringing into sharper focus 'the kind of ministers that God calls and the Church needs to serve the Gospel today and tomorrow'.[19] These perspectives were those of serving Jesus Christ (theological), serving within a changing society (sociological) and the Church's own experience of ministry in a wide range of contexts (ecclesiological). The ministry of word and sacrament was examined within the context of the ministry of the whole people of God and the integration of ministerial person and function commended. 'In those called to this particular ordained ministry the Church should discern a mature and growing integration of person and practice, being and function, as two related aspects of the one life lived in Christ's grace and service.'[20] It is not possible to do justice to this substantial report here, but it is relevant to emphasise three key words, or 'working axioms', in connection with ministry today. These are 'collaborative', 'reflective' and 'formative'.

Reference was made earlier to the old idea of the parish minister as a solo operator. In time past ministers did not move charges with anything like the frequency they do today and many did not move at all. Memorial plaques in old churches testify to ministries of fifty and sixty years. Such longevity, added to the social and natural authority vested in the office, gives a strong sense of such old-time clerics as ecclesiastical masters of all they surveyed. Today the emphasis is much more on team ministry. Whether in an officially formalised staff team such as minister, associate, deacon and youth worker, or in a single-handed ministry in harness with session clerk, elders, organist, Sunday School leaders, etc., the emphasis is on collaboration. Just as a breakdown in such critical relationships can lead a congregation into an unsatisfactory state, so the positive development of such relationships can give great energy and creativity to the life of church and community. It also releases the minister to concentrate on the things which he or she is particularly called and qualified to do, such as preaching, leadership of worship, Bible study and pastoral care. If the Church is to maintain its commitment to a territorial ministry, and engage effectively in mission and service, then ministerial resources need to be harnessed strategically and productively and this is best done in a healthy team setting.

The idea of reflective ministry relates, self-evidently, to an ability to learn from experience. We live in a time of great change and many ministers are called to lead congregations through times of change. Change can be painful and traumatic. For example, few things in the life of the Church cause more distress than the struggle to come to terms with the loss of a familiar church building. Indeed, faced with such a loss many members have severed their links with the Church altogether. How very sad that discipleship should be so linked to stone and mortar! How much better it would be if church people could reflect together on changing social realities, and develop a shared vision of new evangelical opportunities in their community. The report observed that

> if ordained ministers are to respond to the changing context of the Church's mission in a changing Scotland and wider world, then they will have to be people with the capacity and gifts for such reflective practice and leadership, exercised in the collaborative setting of the shared ministry of the whole Church.[21]

The third working axiom identified by the report is 'formative' ministry. What this expresses is the concern that, having collaborated in and reflected upon ministry, all those involved should allow the experience to shape their future growth and development. As the report put it: 'Those called to be ministers of the gospel must be open to continuing formation in the attributes that their office and service require.'[22] In other words, what is envisaged is a process through which the Church nurtures the formation of all its members in the Christian life and out of this emerge those with the gifts and maturity of life and faith to serve as ministers. In this way the ordained ministry of word and sacrament and the ministry of the whole Church grow together in faith and service.

One very practical sign of the Church's commitment to continuing ministerial formation has been the introduction of the study leave scheme. Pioneered by the larger presbyteries this provision is now available to all ministers. After a period of years of service the minister is given time away from the regular round of pastoral duties so that he or she can reflect on a topic of personal interest and professional relevance. In 1991 I was a grateful participant in Glasgow Presbytery's recently introduced scheme and spent three months in the United States and Canada. There I attended a variety of church assemblies and met with officials in a number of denominations to discuss issues of church polity and government. I was also able to take in some continuing education courses which are mandatory for many American clergy, with time off provided for attendance over and above holiday entitlement. In our own country many professionals are familiar with the concept of continuing professional development (CPD). Should the Church's ministry be any different in this regard if it is to have fresh insights and new thoughts to share with the membership?

OTHER MINISTRIES

The focus of this chapter has been on the ministry of word and sacrament, also known as the parish ministry. However, this is not the only ministry within the Church and if the concept of collaboration means anything then it means these various ministries, literally, working together. There exist within the Church various offices and it will be helpful to say a brief word about each of these.

Reference has already been made to the Auxiliary Ministry in Chapter 2. We saw there that this ministry was one of the practical outcomes of the deliberations of the Committee of Forty in the 1970s. It allows for people working in other jobs, or retired, to undergo appropriate training, leading to ordination to a ministry of word and sacrament, which is exercised on a part-time and non-stipendiary basis. This ministry is supportive of and complementary to the whole-time ministry and is crucial in supplying 'the ordinances of religion to the people in every parish of Scotland through a territorial ministry'.

An ancient office in the Church is that of reader. In the immediate aftermath of the Reformation there was a shortage of ministers and it often fell to someone such as the local school teacher to read prayers and passages of Scripture until the minister arrived to preach the sermon. The office as we now know it provides an opportunity for church members to undertake training which will equip them to prepare and preach sermons. Readers are 'set apart' to this office and exercise a valuable preaching ministry, sometimes within team ministries, but also being available to provide pulpit supply to cover ministerial absence. Many 'lay' people have valuable experiences and insights derived from their life in the world and it is good that these can be shared through this ministry.

Two offices, no longer extant as such, are lay missionary and deaconess. My own grandfather was a lay missionary with the Home Board (precursor of the Board of National Mission). A Gaelic-speaking crofter/fisherman, he exercised a gentle and influential ministry in Skye, Sutherland and his own native Lewis. Such men (for men they were) complemented the work of the parish minister, leading Bible study, conducting prayer meetings and services and generally sharing in the work of pastoral care.

A similar role was exercised on the female side by deaconesses. At one time also known as church sisters, the first deaconess, Lady Grisell Baillie, was appointed in the parish of Bowden in 1888, part of the renewing strategy associated with the name of Dr Archibald Charteris, which also gave the Church the Woman's Guild and *Life & Work*. In the period following the Second World War many of these women gave marvellous service, for example, in the new housing-scheme parishes which grew up around the large cities and towns of Scotland. I have impressive memories of the team of minister and deaconess at Camperdown Parish Church in Dundee in the early 1960s, Peter Gordon and May Robertson, with whom I served as a very youthful church organist. The distinctive grey uniform and hat of the deaconess was as familiar and respected a badge of office as the minister's clerical collar.

Traditionally lay missionaries were exclusively male whereas deaconesses, as the term indicates, were female. In 1988 the two 'orders' merged to form what today is known as the Diaconate,[23] with its members known by the gender-inclusive title of deacons.[24] In 2001 the Board of

Ministry followed up its previous year's report, 'Ministers of the Gospel', with a complementary document entitled 'Deacons of the Gospel'. This began with a generous 'recognition of the distinctive ministry of the Diaconate and its vital role in the changing patterns of ministry in the life of the Church of Scotland today'.[25] The diaconal ministry certainly complements the ministry of word and sacrament, with deacons, largely though not exclusively, working in team situations. Since 2002 deacons have been ordained, whereas formerly they were commissioned. The General Assembly of 2003 supported a call that the implications of a deacon being in charge of a parish and also the possibility of deacons being authorised to conduct weddings should be explored.

As well as these distinctive ministries of deacon, auxiliary and reader it is also important to mention the eldership, often referred to as one of the great strengths of the Presbyterian tradition. The *Second Book of Discipline* (1581) describes the eldership as 'a spiritual office' and, consistent with this, elders like ministers and deacons are ordained. The Church has around 40,000 elders, a formidable force for good, both within the Church and the wider community. The elders, with the minister, form the Kirk Session, the local church court with spiritual oversight of the congregation and parish. The pastoral aspect of the office is exercised through the elder's district. As previously noted, there was a time when the purpose of the elder's visit was to catechise and examine the people to ensure that they were fit to receive Communion. While the visit today is still largely associated with the Sacrament, and the delivery of Communion cards, its essential focus is pastoral – an expression of Christian interest in the individual or family and an encouragement to their participation in the life of the congregation. In my own parish ministry I was always grateful to the elders for their quarterly contact with church families and their passing on of matters of concern, with the suggestion that I might follow them up as minister. This was team ministry at its very best.

While, as noted above, the eldership is regarded as one of the Kirk's great strengths, there is a continuing debate as to whether the Church makes the best use of this considerable human resource. The principle of ordination for life has traditionally been taken to mean active service on a Kirk Session for life. In many cases this has been a source of blessing, but it can also lead to unhelpful issues of power, control and conflict within congregations seeking to address issues of change, perhaps under the guidance of a new minister. The sense of a commitment for life can also be a deterrent in recruiting new elders and, in my view, there is much to be said for allowing, if not actually requiring, elders to take a break after a period of years. This would allow people to make a contribution and then step, honourably, aside without feeling they were letting the side down. It would also allow many Kirk Sessions to become self-renewing, as distinct from self-perpetuating. The new Unitary Constitution introduced in 2003 as an alternative to the Model Constitution[26] allows for a more flexible approach, utilising the gifts of those who are not elders in committees, pastoral care and short-term projects, while leaving ultimate responsibility for the congregation's well-being with the Session.

While gladly affirming the importance of healthy collaboration among all who exercise the Church's various and varied ministries I must also mention a tension in the General Assembly of 2002, of which I was Moderator, and upon which I reflected in my concluding address to that year's Assembly. This related to two separate issues which generated some controversy and raised questions about the relative roles of ministers and elders within the Church.

The issue first arose on the report of the Board of Parish Education and had to do with the leadership of worship in the absence of the minister. An Act of 1986 provided for this and specified the various categories of people who were authorised so to deputise. They included such obvious groups as retired ministers, divinity students, deacons, readers and auxiliary ministers. There was also a general provision to a presbytery to approve a scheme involving others where this was required. It was apparent that this latter provision was being interpreted generously and that, in some areas, presbyteries were authorising elders, following some basic training, to conduct worship and to preach. The Board now proposed to regularise such arrangements. There was resistance on the grounds that, if elders could be authorised to occupy pulpits after a few evening classes, why should people undergo the demanding training required for the readership and auxiliary ministry, not to mention several years of full-time study, to prepare for the ministry of word and sacrament? In a rather tetchy debate some emphasised the value of a professional ministry while others stressed the need not to stifle the spiritual gifts of elders. In the event the proposals of the Board of Parish Education carried.

The other issue was raised by the Board of Ministry. Worried about the excessive burdens placed upon parish ministers it sought to relieve some of these by proposing that suitable elders be permitted to act as interim moderators in vacancies. After all, an elder could be appointed as moderator of presbytery, or even General Assembly. Why not a Kirk Session in a vacancy situation? Again the question arose as to what tasks and functions within a collaborative culture ought properly to be reserved to the 'professionals'. If the Church was seriously concerned about recruiting able and committed men and women into the full-time ministry then, surely, these men and women should have a clear job to do, a job which only they could do. Not so, said others. We must eschew such elitism. Surely an elder with relevant experience of chairing meetings and conducting business was perfectly capable of presiding at a Kirk Session meeting, and if by doing so a busy parish minister was spared a fifty-mile round trip on a winter's night, so much the better! Again, the innovators prevailed and the following year, 2003, the General Assembly went further and approved an Overture which would allow an elder to preside at a regular Session meeting, in the absence of the minister, rather than the minister being required to find another minister to take his or her place. The concern of many remains that, while there is practical wisdom in making best use of ministerial resources, care must also be taken not to undervalue the mindset and 'hinterland' of those who have immersed themselves in three years of theological education, studied the Scriptures in depth, acquired an understanding of the sweep of church history and responded to a serious and sacrificial call to full-time ministry. It is also recognised that the Church has not always harnessed the resources of the eldership to their fullest potential and, certainly, we are a long way from saying that anyone can do everything. Nevertheless, from a ministerial point of view, warning bells have been sounded.

There is also the matter of recruitment to the whole-time ministry. One of the success stories of recent years has been the Enquirers' Conference. These annual gatherings bring together all who have expressed an interest in full-time service to the Church. Not all are thinking of ministry. Some are contemplating work overseas, or Christian social work, or education. In the course of a twenty-four-hour residential conference they are introduced to the various facets of the Church's life and given an informed opportunity to work out whether the promptings which have brought them this far have the makings of a call. At the same time the question has been raised as to whether, having regard to financial constraints, any limit should be set upon the Church's recruitment ambitions. Should thought be given, for example, to setting an affordable upper limit to the numbers of full-time ministers, with such a professional ministry deployed strategically in leadership roles around the country, supporting and enabling teams of elders, deacons, auxiliaries and readers as appropriate? Or, is that an exercise in faithlessness and a failure truly to believe that God will supply the Church's needs and provide the Church with the resources to meet those needs?

What is clear is that ministry has changed much over the years. It is equally certain that it will continue to evolve in ways which meet the needs of the contemporary church and our wider society. Jesus Christ came 'not to be served but to serve'[27] and in that same spirit men and women will continue to come forward, responding to Christ's call and working together in the service of his Church.

NOTES

1 Articles Declaratory of the Constitution of the Church of Scotland in Matters Spiritual, Article III.
2 J. T. Cox, *Practice and Procedure in the Church of Scotland*, 6th edn, ed. D. F. M. MacDonald, Edinburgh: Church of Scotland, 1976, p. 55.
3 The diaconate here refers to membership of the Deacons' Court, the body which administered the financial affairs of many congregations.
4 Assembly Papers, 1931, p. 63.
5 See General Assembly Reports, 1959, pp. 795–813.

6 The Reverend Mary Levison records her story in *Wrestling with the Church*, Arthur James, 1992.

7 Verbatim Minutes of the General Assembly, 1967, p. 123.

8 Assembly Reports, 1991, p. 5.

9 Assembly Reports, 1996, p. 23/2.

10 See Assembly Reports, 2002, p. 1/32.

11 Assembly Reports, 2002, p. 1/32.

12 J. H. S. Burleigh, *A Church History of Scotland*, London: Oxford University Press, 1960, p. 315.

13 Assembly Reports, 1987, p. 210.

14 Assembly Reports, 1987, p. 210.

15 Assembly Reports, 1993, p. 297.

16 Assembly Reports, 1996, p. 14/12.

17 For the sake of completeness it should be noted that an Act of the General Assembly of 1984, anent Congregations in Changed Circumstances allows a presbytery to dissolve the pastoral tie if circumstances have changed so much since the minister's induction as to render the charge non-viable. However, this piece of legislation has never been used.

18 Assembly Reports, 2000, p. 17/3.

19 Assembly Reports, 2000, p. 17/5.

20 Assembly Reports, 2000, p. 17/9.

21 Assembly Reports, 2000, p. 17/23.

22 Assembly Reports, 2000, p. 17/23.

23 The diaconate or diakonal (serving) ministry is an ancient one. At the time of the Reformation deacons were essentially church treasurers (see Burleigh, *Church History*, p. 172), but also assisted the minister and elders more generally. The office largely died out in the eighteenth century.

24 For the avoidance of confusion it should be noted that the term 'deacon' is also used in a different sense to refer to members of a Deacons' Court (see note 3 above). In some congregations of the United Free tradition this name is still used of the Financial Court, rather than 'Congregational Board'.

25 Assembly Reports, 2001, p. 17/3.

26 The Model Constitution provides for a Kirk Session with responsibility for 'matters spiritual' and a Congregational Board, comprising elders and elected members who are not elders, with responsibility for 'matters temporal'. Under the Unitary Constitution there is no Congregational Board, the Kirk Session having responsibility for both aspects.

27 Mark 10:45.

7

Changing Attitudes: Ecumenism

ECUMENISM AND MOVES TOWARDS CHURCH REUNION

In his *Church History of Scotland*, published in 1960 to mark the four-hundredth anniversary of the Scottish Reformation, Professor J. H. S. Burleigh describes the ecumenical movement as 'the most impressive event in recent church history'.[1] Burleigh traces the origin of the movement to a World Missionary Conference held in Edinburgh in 1910 in what is now the Church of Scotland's Assembly Hall. This gathering was attended by delegates from churches and missionary societies from around the globe with the purpose of developing a co-operative approach to world-wide evangelism. After all, it was the Gospel that disciples were to proclaim to the ends of the earth, not particular forms of denominational organisation.

The word 'ecumenical' is derived from the Greek *oikoumenikos*. The term means 'of the inhabited world' and expresses the sense of the Church as one in all the earth. In the seventeenth chapter of St John's Gospel we read of Jesus praying that his followers might be one. We know that the history of the Church over the two intervening millennia has been very different. On occasions Christians have even resorted to appalling violence against their fellow believers, absurdly claiming this to be in the name of gospel truth. We need look no further than our own borders for dreadful examples where still, today, the monster of sectarianism refuses to lie down and die.

We have also noted, more hopefully, that, while the seventeenth, eighteenth and early nineteenth centuries saw secession and disruption in Scottish church life, the late nineteenth and twentieth centuries brought reconciliation and union. It is hard, today, to believe that between 1847 and 1900, what we now know as the Church of Scotland was split three ways into the Established Church of Scotland, the Free Church and the United Presbyterian Church. There is an ecclesiastical joke, set in a small Scottish town, where all three denominations were represented. Over three successive evenings each congregation held a meeting in the burgh hall. On the first night the members of the Church of Scotland met. A banner over the stage proclaimed, 'Zion shall be established'. On the following evening it was the turn of the Free Church. Their banner asserted, 'The truth shall make you free'. Finally, it was the turn of the United Presbyterian congregation. They, too, had their distinctive banner which announced, 'The tribes of God go UP'. All joking apart, however, these divisions ran very deep and we should never underestimate the ecumenical endeavour which went into the mere healing of Scotland's fractured Presbyterian family. Today, ecumenism covers a far wider spectrum, bringing together Presbyterian and Episcopalian, Methodist and Baptist, Catholic and Orthodox – not into any structural unification, but at least into dialogue and a sharing of witness and service.

As long ago as 1581, *The Second Book of Discipline*, after referring to 'the nationall assemblie (quhilk is generall to us)' goes on to describe

> an uther mair generall kind of assemblie quhilk [which] is of all nations or of all estatis of personis within the kirk representing the universall kirk of Chryst quhilk may be callit properlie the generall assemblie or generall counsall of the haill [whole] kirk of God.[2]

This is a remarkable statement and shows great vision on the part of those who were seeking to reform the Scottish church in the late sixteenth century. They were driven by no narrow nationalism but by a desire for a Church in all the world that truly represented the values of the Gospel.

In the same spirit, those who, in the early years of the twentieth century, framed the Declaratory Articles, which still express the basic constitution of the Church of Scotland, gave prominent place to the ecumenical dimension. These Articles clearly set out the Kirk's commitment to Reformed doctrine and Presbyterian government. They also recognised 'the obligation to seek and promote union with other Churches in which [the Church of Scotland] finds the Word to be purely preached, the sacraments administered according to Christ's ordinance and discipline rightly exercised'.[3] It should be noted, however, that with the exception of the accession of the Original Secession Church to the Church of Scotland in 1956 no such union has occurred.

This is not for want of trying. In the 1970s the prospect of a union involving the Church of Scotland and the Methodist Synods of Scotland and Shetland was explored. A Basis and Plan of Union was approved by the General Assembly of 1978 and, thereafter, by a majority of presbyteries. However, the following year the Assembly learned that the Methodist Church had felt unable to agree to this, with the result that the proposal fell. In departing from the matter the General Assembly of 1979 encouraged presbyteries and congregations 'to engage in as much contact and co-operation as possible with Methodist congregations in their areas'.

Meanwhile, in 1968, five churches accepted the Church of Scotland's invitation to begin working towards the unity of the Christian Church in Scotland. The five were the Churches of Christ (later to become part of the United Reformed Church), the Congregational Union of Scotland, the Methodist Church, the Scottish Episcopal Church and the United Free Church. The Baptist and Roman Catholic Churches appointed observers to the ensuing 'Multilateral Church Conversation'. The conversation continued for the next twenty-five years, producing a number of reports which testified to a growing agreement on points of doctrine and a recognition that matters on which there was disagreement were not of such magnitude as to warrant continuing separation.

The Conversation stopped short of bringing forward firm proposals for a structural union of the participating churches. Rather, in its final 1992 report, entitled *Who Goes Where?*, it sought a new mandate for the next phase. Confidently, the report asserted:

> Our task is clear. We are to discover how to bring our churches together, so that members and ministries are reconciled and mutually recognised, in order to pursue effective common witness and service within the wider jurisdiction of a united church.

The Scottish Episcopal Church took up the challenge in a paper entitled, *Who Goes Forward with Us?* This document set out changes in that Church's life and practice, such as the ordination of women and an understanding of the office of bishop as sign, rather than guarantee, of the Church's unity and continuity. Arguing that these changes addressed matters which had created difficulties for some other churches, the Scottish Episcopal Church invited its fellow participants in the Multilateral Conversations to join it in direct negotiations for a formal union. Five out of the six accepted, the United Free Church being the exception. So it came about that in January 1996, a new process began under the title The Scottish Church Initiative for Union. SCIFU, as it came to be known, built on the work of the previous thirty years of conversations, but now had in view the very clear goal of a united church. A target date of 2010 was even suggested – a fitting way of celebrating the centenary of the Edinburgh Missionary Conference.

However, it was not to be; at least not involving all five participants. The SCIFU negotiators made good progress, agreeing documents on a range of matters such as ministry, local church organisation, church government and mission. Two interim reports were prepared and debated widely within the participating churches. In an encouraging development the Scottish Congregational Union united with the United Reformed Church in 2000 and became the Scottish National Synod of that Church, itself a union forged in 1972 between the Presbyterian Church of England and the Congregational Church in England and Wales. Less encouragingly, that same year SCIFU's second interim report received a rather rough ride in the General Assembly of the Church of Scotland. The Committee on Ecumenical Relations faced a challenge in the form of a counter-motion which asked that the Assembly, 'recognising the vital importance of Christian unity, cherish the diversity of Christian witness in Scotland, and do not believe that institutional union is either necessary or desirable at this time, and instruct the committee to cease participation in SCIFU'. After a full and passionate debate this counter-motion was defeated by 276 votes to 238. The closeness of the vote was not a good omen and, finally, in 2003, following a decisive vote in the General Assembly, the Church of

Scotland withdrew from the process, leaving the remaining participants to go forward. With a membership ten times that of the other churches combined, there was no denying that the withdrawal of the Kirk was a very serious blow.

The 2003 General Assembly debate reflected suspicions and concerns over the shape of the proposed new church. The idea of the 'maxi-parish' seemed vague and undermining of local church identity, efforts to reconcile Presbyterian, Episcopal and Congregational systems appeared overly bureaucratic and, in general, the majority was simply not persuaded that the pursuit of organic union would do anything to strengthen the missionary endeavours of the churches. The motion which carried the day in the 2003 Assembly noted 'the valuable work carried out by all involved in the SCIFU discussions over the past seven years'. It then went on to acknowledge 'that the growing spirit of unity among Christians in Scotland is unlikely to be advanced by implementing the SCIFU proposals' and instructed the Ecumenical Relations Committee to withdraw from further involvement with the process. The seventh Declaratory Article certainly speaks of an obligation to seek and promote unity. However, it also qualifies the Kirk's right to enter into a union by requiring that such union must not involve loss of identity and that it should be on terms that the Church finds to be consistent with the Declaratory Articles. While such specific questions were not debated in the Assembly, it was apparent that the majority believed that too much would be conceded, were the Kirk to have continued in the process. Nevertheless, before moving on to the next business the Assembly did 'reaffirm its commitment to visible union with other Churches in the spirit of Article VII of its Articles Declaratory' and urged 'congregations, with the help and guidance of the (Ecumenical Relations) Committee, to engage with neighbouring churches of other denominations (and their own) by establishing and operating Local Ecumenical Partnerships wherever this is possible'.

Reference has already been made to the speech by the Reverend Paraic Raemonn,[4] a committed ecumenist and staff member of the Geneva-based World Alliance of Reformed Churches. He argued that the SCIFU proposals were flawed in that they were based on an outdated model of ecumenism. It is certainly the case that much contemporary ecumenical activity is focused not on the organic union of churches but on the principle, known as the Lund principle,[5] of churches doing together what they did not need to do separately. It is relevant to note that in 1990 the former Scottish Churches' Council was wound up and replaced by a new ecumenical instrument known as Action of Churches Together in Scotland (ACTS). The new name says it all. The equivalent body south of the border is known as Churches Together in England (CTE) and the UK Britain and Ireland instrument is Churches Together in Britain and Ireland (CTBI). Again the word 'together' is crucial.

The formation of these new ecumenical instruments was also significant because of the willingness of the Roman Catholic Church to become part of them, having opted only for observer status on the former councils. The visit to Britain by the Pope in 1982, with his call to walk 'hand in hand' and the launching of the Inter-Church Process 'Not Strangers but Pilgrims' in 1984 gave a new energy to ecumenical effort. This found powerful expression in the 'Swanwick Declaration' of September 1987, agreed at Swanwick, Derbyshire, by the broadest Assembly of British and Irish churches ever to meet in these islands. This affirmed a readiness 'to commit ourselves to each other under God' and expressed a desire to 'become more fully, in (God's) own time, the one Church of Christ, united in faith, communion, pastoral care and mission'. At the same time the Declaration recognised that 'in the unity we seek . . . there will not be uniformity but legitimate diversity'. It is not always easy to tell which is cause and which effect, but, arguably, the atmosphere which facilitated Swanwick and produced the Declaration was itself the result of a gradual breaking down of barriers of separation and distrust at local level, through such initiatives as the Week of Prayer for Christian Unity, shared Holy Week services and the like.

Some felt that the outcome of the SCIFU process did not reflect well on the Church of Scotland and, arguably, it does raise questions about the seriousness with which the Church takes its obligations under the seventh Declaratory Article, to which reference has been made more than once. That said, the fact remains that in terms of ecumenical friendship and co-operation with other churches the Kirk has a good track record. Not only is it the major financial contributor to ACTS it is the second biggest contributor to CTBI and also plays a prominent role in international ecumenical bodies such as the World Council of Churches (WCC), the World Alliance of Reformed Churches (WARC) and the Council of European Churches (CEC).

MODERATORS AND POPES

The Kirk has also taken various initiatives to foster good ecumenical relations within Scotland. In 1961 the question was raised in the General Assembly as to whether the Moderator, who was due to visit Rome, should seek to pay a courtesy call on the Pope. It is a measure of how much things have changed that it is not easy today fully to grasp the radical nature of this suggestion. The proposal itself was couched in very cautious terms, seeking merely permission 'to consider the advisability of the Moderator, when in Rome, paying a courtesy visit to the Pope; and, if thought advisable, to make the necessary arrangements'.[6] (Note, it was made clear that the Moderator was going to be in Rome anyway; he wasn't going especially to see the Pope!) No less than three Assembly Committees (General Administration, Colonial and Continental and Inter-Church Relations) were involved in discussions, and the decision to proceed was taken at a joint meeting of all three. This decision was based on the recognition that it was desirable to promote better relationships between Protestants and Roman Catholics in Scotland and overseas and a sense that, despite wide doctrinal differences, many in the Church would welcome such a visit 'as a step to friendlier relations between members of the Churches involved ... since Christian charity could be manifested, goodwill fostered and no truth safeguarded by the Church of Scotland compromised by a courtesy visit by the Moderator of the General Assembly to the Vatican, any invitation from the Pope to pay such a visit should be warmly accepted'.[7] The visit by the Right Reverend Dr Archie Craig duly took place amid much interest and publicity. In reporting on it to the General Assembly of 1962 Dr Craig recalled a discussion in which someone had said, 'We must speak the truth and we have some hard things to say to the Roman Catholics.'

Someone else then remarked, 'Yes, certainly, but we must learn to speak the truth in love, even when it is a hard truth.' A third person then observed, 'Remember, you can't either speak the truth, or speak it in love, unless you begin to speak.' In light of these comments Dr Craig expressed the hope that his meeting with the Pope had 'helped to create the beginnings of a climate for that necessary dialogue and to set . . . a pattern of courtesy, sincerity and charity'. If so, 'then surely, under God's guidance, and in God's way and in God's time, it shall not have been entirely fruitless'.[8] Humour also came into it. A joke circulating at the time asked what was the Pope's farewell greeting to Moderator Archie Craig. The answer: 'Arrivederci Erchie!'

In the event, the dialogue begun by Dr Craig developed so vigorously that in 1968 the Inter-Church Relations Committee could report that 'one of the encouraging signs of the present is the new climate of understanding and goodwill which is developing between the Roman Catholic Church and other Communions'.[9] By way of illustration the Committee cited the fact that Church of Scotland observers had attended the Second Vatican Council in 1963. Building on this, the Committee now proposed that the Roman Catholic Church in Scotland be invited, formally, to send a Visitor to the next Assembly. This proposal was approved and in 1969 Father Jock Dalrymple was welcomed in this official capacity. This precedent, happily established, continued from year to year until 1991 when the status of the Roman Catholic representative at the Assembly was raised to that of delegate, the crucial difference being that a delegate is entitled to speak, though not to vote. Now it is quite customary for the Roman Catholic delegate to contribute as appropriate to Assembly debates. For example, much merriment was occasioned in 2002 by Archbishop Keith Patrick O'Brien's gentle fun-poking at the bench of former Moderators, to whom he referred as a 'college of cardinals'. And, in October 2003, when the Archbishop was elevated to the office of Cardinal, the Church of Scotland was well represented, at his specific request, among those invited to the ceremonies and celebrations in Rome.

In 1975 another important step was taken in developing relations between the Church of Scotland and the Roman Catholic Church, when

Archbishop Thomas Winning of Glasgow, the Invited Visitor that year, addressed the General Assembly. In his speech Archbishop Winning spoke of 'a bridge being built, centuries being spanned, a silence of 415 years being broken and friendships being renewed'.[10] He asked, 'What do brothers say to one another after years – and, in our case, centuries of silence? Surely, they ask forgiveness.'[11] He then went on to quote, and own for himself, the Pope's words at the Second Vatican Council:

> If we are in any way to blame for [the long years of] separation, we humbly beg God's forgiveness. And we ask pardon, too, of our brethren [sic] who feel themselves to have been injured by us. For our part we willingly forgive the injuries which the Catholic Church has suffered, and forget the grief endured during the long series of dissensions and separations.

The Archbishop concluded by expressing his commitment to work with the Church of Scotland and other Christian Churches towards unity. In reply the Moderator, Dr James Matheson, also in ecumenical vein, quoted words of the founder of Methodism, John Wesley: 'I don't say, come over to my side, nor drive me to thine, but if my heart is as thine heart with the love of Christ, then give me thy hand.' In a movingly significant act Dr Matheson then invited all to stand and say the doxology together – *Glory be to the Father and to the Son and to the Holy Ghost; as it was in the beginning, is now and shall be evermore, Amen.*

Seven years later, in June 1982, the Pope, during the course of his visit to Scotland, paid a courtesy call on the Moderator, Professor John McIntyre. The two men met and greeted one another cordially in the quadrangle of the Assembly Hall at New College. There was not a little wry amusement that this historic encounter took place beneath the statue of John Knox. A month previously the General Assembly had received a petition from the Free Presbyterian Church urging that the meeting should not take place and this found some support within the Assembly. However, the vote in favour was overwhelming. In recent years Andrew McLellan (Moderator 2000) and John Miller (Moderator 2001) met Pope John Paul II and, during the course of his Moderatorial year (1978–9), Peter Brodie, accompanied by Principal Clerk Donald Macdonald, was a guest of the Scottish hierarchy at the inauguration ceremonies of Popes John Paul I and John Paul II.

Further evidence of changing attitudes in Church of Scotland/Roman Catholic relations can be found in an Overture brought to the General Assembly of 1986 by Dr Kenneth Stewart, an elder from Stirling. This asked the Assembly to declare that the Church no longer affirmed certain phrases in the Westminster Confession of Faith which reflected a seventeenth-century Protestant way of referring to the Roman Catholic Church. Dr Stewart argued that language which spoke of 'infidels, papists and other idolators' and described the pope as 'Antichrist, that Man of Sin and Perdition' represented 'a continuing offence' and were 'beyond modification except by their exclusion'. The General Assembly agreed and passed an Act dissociating itself from such statements and declaring that it did not require its office-bearers to believe in them.

In 1999 the same kind of issue arose when the Scottish Parliament debated the continuing appropriateness of the Act of Settlement, an Act of Parliament dating back to 1701 which prohibits the heir to the throne from marrying a Roman Catholic. The Church of Scotland was asked for a view and this was offered by the Board of Practice and Procedure and reported to the General Assembly of 2000.[12] The Board expressed the opinion that the Act was a product of its times and that its discriminatory provisions had no place in contemporary society. While acknowledging the constitutional complexities the Board argued that the Church should not oppose any proposal to review the Act. At the same time, the Board went on to remark that

> it would be a matter of regret to the Church of Scotland were a Roman Catholic Sovereign to be put into a position of denying the validity of Church of Scotland orders and of being prevented by Roman Catholic discipline from receiving communion within the Church of Scotland, or indeed within other Protestant and Reformed Churches within the United Kingdom.

Such encounters and episodes reflect the public face of ecumenism and they illustrate well a growing spirit of ecumenical friendship and co-operation. However, it is important also to note the growth of quiet sharing at congregational level through local ecumenical projects and councils of churches. Shared Bible study, Christian Aid collections and other such activities have increasingly brought people from different church traditions together. In my own ministry I shared on a number of occasions in what were commonly referred to as 'mixed marriages', both in my own church with a priest assisting and in a Roman Catholic marriage service where I assisted the priest – and this has, indeed, become increasingly common.

LIVINGSTON AND OTHER LOCAL ECUMENICAL INITIATIVES

If one were to name one Scottish town which is particularly associated with ecumenism that town would be Livingston. The stimulus for the Multilateral Church Conversations already referred to came from the Faith and Order Conference held in Nottingham in 1964. This gathering of representatives of twenty-four British Churches explored the themes of Unity, Renewal and Mission and became an important energy source for ecumenical activity, though looking back its aspirations of a united Church, not later than Easter Day 1980, was wildly optimistic. Nottingham also provided the inspiration for an idea that new towns be designated areas of ecumenical experiment. Accordingly, in 1965 the General Assembly set up a Special Committee to consider the implications of this proposal and the following year it was agreed that Livingston should be so designated. The Church of Scotland, the Scottish Episcopal Church and the Congregational Union of Scotland would enter into agreements that new buildings would be denominationally owned, but that hospitality within them would be extended to the other two churches. For the Church of Scotland the experiment would be monitored by the Presbytery of Livingston and Bathgate (now West Lothian) and the Home Board's National Church Extension Committee. By 1968 the Methodist Church had become part of the experiment and, that same year the Bishop of Edinburgh gave permission for members of the other denominations to share in the Scottish Episcopal Eucharist. By 1975 the inter-denominational staff team comprised two Church of Scotland ministers, two Scottish Episcopal priests, one Congregational minister and a Methodist deaconess. A new Ecumenical Council was also in place to facilitate the administration of the experiment, though the traditional bodies associated with the participating churches – presbytery, bishop, conference – also continued to have a role.

In 1982 the General Assembly appointed a Special Commission, subsequently enlarged to include representatives from the other Churches, to review the experiment. Two years later this reported and its recommendations included a change of name from 'Livingston Ecumenical Experiment' to 'Livingston Ecumenical Parish' and also that the project should continue for at least a further five years with the same staffing complement. A new Sponsors' Council was also put in place and asked to bring a report in 1989 recommending 'continuance, revision or termination of the project'. This report, while recommending continuance, expressed some frustration over uncertainties arising from the complex ecumenical and denominational structures involved in decision-making. The report of the Ecumenical Relations Committee to the 2003 Assembly refers to the same problem which it describes as 'a fragmented way of working', though the Committee also speaks positively of 'community outreach initiatives and faith nurturing programmes which show that there is much life at the heart of this parish'.[13] However, the frustrations of the Presbytery of West Lothian also surfaced at the same Assembly with an Overture (unsuccessful) asking for a Commission 'to consider how best the Church of Scotland could make a more significant contribution to the life of the Church within the area of Livingston Ecumenical Parish'.

There are certainly differing opinions on the effectiveness of the Livingston 'experiment'. However, one thing which is very apparent is the commitment of the Church of Scotland to new ways of working appropriate to an ecumenical age. In this and in other situations the General Assembly has displayed both flexibility and creativity in allowing new things to happen. For example, in 1991 the General Assembly granted a petition from three Paisley congregations, two Church of Scotland and one Congregational, seeking permission to unite and become a congregation in membership of both denominations. The enabling legislation provided for both a Congregational Meeting and for a Kirk Session, with each member of the ministerial team, whether Church of Scotland or Congregationalist, authorised to act as moderator. Indeed, the following year, the General Assembly passed a more general Act authorising ministers of other denominations, serving in an ecumenical parish of which the Church of Scotland was part, to act as Moderator of the Kirk Session. Special arrangements have also been made in places as different as Morningside and Jura to allow ministers of other denominations to have seats in presbytery. The function of church law, practice and procedure is to enable and not to frustrate. Certainly, time taken to get things right can be frustrating, but it is always better that things be done 'decently and in order'. The Church of Scotland has shown flair, imagination and flexibility in this whole area.

Quite apart from these institutional examples there is also a greatly changed climate at the local level. Ministers' fellowship meetings are now invariably fully ecumenical, pulpit exchanges across denominational lines are common and those associated with presbyteries at ministerial inductions will usually cover the local ecumenical spectrum. Local ecumenical friendships develop and flourish, with or without any official sanction or recognition. One such arose quite spontaneously in the course of my ministry in Jordanhill and is a story worth the telling.

In the summer of 1990 our congregation held a flower festival as part of a series of events to celebrate Glasgow's year as European City of Culture. A member of the congregation, a builder who looked after the monastery home of a closed order of Carmelite nuns, had told the sisters of our plans. Their response was to send bunches of flowers from their beautiful garden as a gift to the festival. This gift was gratefully received and I was dispatched to say 'thank you'.

I was somewhat uncertain as to what to expect, never having visited a closed order of nuns. I was told that I would be shown into an austere parlour which would be divided by a grille. The nuns would be on one side and I would be on the other. I thought, 'This won't take long.' How wrong I was. For over an hour we talked and laughed together. When it was time for me to leave, the prioress and I joined hands through the grille and we each said a short prayer. I departed with an invitation to return with members of my congregation, perhaps for a shared act of worship.

So it happened that a pattern established itself, which continues to the present day. Three or four times a year, usually to mark seasons such as Advent, Lent, Easter, Harvest, shared worship is offered in the lovely monastery chapel, worship that is not only offered together but planned and prepared together by the nuns and members of the Jordanhill congregation.

When the time came for me to leave Glasgow the nuns gave me a gift of a preaching stole, designed and made by one of them who had previously been a fashion designer. Sister Teresa Margaret and I discussed appropriate symbols for the stole and came up with an image which combines the burning bush and the Celtic cross, thereby connecting God's power and God's love and celebrating our shared origins as Scottish Christians, long before the days of Catholic and Protestant.

Much of the foregoing has dealt with Church of Scotland/Roman Catholic relationships and this is appropriate, given the continuing problem of sectarianism. Much has been made recently of the sectarian nature of reports of the Church and Nation Committee in the 1920s with their hostile remarks about Irish Catholic immigration. Harry Reid in *Outside Verdict* goes so far as to describe the Committee's convener of the time, Dr John White (architect of the 1929 union), as 'the Kirk's Bad Man'. In 2002 the General Assembly expressed regret at 'any part played in sectarianism by our Church in the past' and affirmed 'our support for future moves toward a more tolerant society'. The Assembly also reminded the Church that 'sectarianism is not someone else's problem' and encouraged congregations 'to set up local working groups to look at the issue within their own communities'.

It is honest of the Assembly to look at the beam in its own eye, and certainly some of the 1920s statements of the Church and Nation Committee make horrific reading today. However, as the foregoing narrative has shown there is also much in its more recent history in which the Church of Scotland can take pride. Initiatives have been taken, both nationally and locally, and while, sadly, sectarian problems remain, relationships between Scotland's two largest churches have moved forward tremendously over the past forty years. That said, one area of challenge and regret which does remain is the fact that we cannot sit down at the same Communion table. There are complex reasons for this. It is understandably difficult for the Roman Catholic Church to offer the Mass to those who do not share their understanding of the Sacrament. Their view is that inter-communion is simply a papering over of the cracks and that the pain we feel in our separation should spur us all to greater efforts towards unity. Then, having reached that goal, we can share the bread and the wine together. By contrast a Protestant view emphasises the Sacrament as a means of grace and argues that by sharing together at what is, after all, the Lord's and not the Church's Table, we will be led by the Spirit into greater unity.

It is also important to emphasise the development of closer relations among all the churches through the various ecumenical conversations and activities referred to. In particular I would mention our relationships with sister Presbyterian churches. The Scottish Churches' Committee, a body which deals with legal matters affecting all the churches, provides a useful forum with a wider membership than ACTS. In recent years also the Free Church, the Free Presbyterian Church and the Associated Presbyterian Church have accepted invitations from the Church of Scotland Moderator to be part of ecumenical and inter-faith visits to the European Union institutions in Brussels and Strasbourg. I welcome this with warmth and enthusiasm.

During the course of the General Assembly of 2003, having laid down my responsibilities as Moderator and not yet resumed the duties of Principal Clerk, I decided to cross the Lawnmarket one afternoon and sit in the public gallery of the Free Church Assembly. I had hoped to do so quietly, even anonymously, but I was recognised and brought downstairs to sit in a side gallery, more within 'the body of the Kirk'. Then, at a suitable point in the proceedings, I was most warmly welcomed by the Moderator, a sentiment which appeared to be endorsed by the commissioners present. The tradition of the Lord High Commissioner paying a courtesy call on the Free Church Assembly continues. How important it is that we hold out the hand of friendship to all who profess to follow Jesus Christ and grasp that same hand when it is extended to us. Truly, to walk hand in hand is a powerful sign of grace that the world might believe.

Finally, in this chapter, I mention the first Scottish Ecumenical Assembly, held in Edinburgh in September 2001. Four hundred people attended from churches all over Scotland and over the course of a weekend explored the theme 'Breaking New Ground'. James Dunn, Professor of New Testament at Durham University, offered a series of reflections based on the challenge to the Church of Jeremiah 1:10 in which the prophet comes to terms with his call 'to uproot and to break down, to destroy and to overthrow, to build and to plant'. Professor Dunn pointed out how this charge to the young prophet offered a timely challenge to churches in weighing the relative priorities of maintaining their denominationalism and joining with others in the task of building and planting. There is a need both for breaking down the things which hinder the unity of God's people, as well as seeking to build that unity, so that the world might believe. The ecumenical imperative continues to find expression in the 'Articles Declaratory of the Constitution of the Church of Scotland in Matters Spiritual'. More than that, all churches need to work ever more closely together in practical service of the Gospel.

NOTES

1 J. H. S. Burleigh, *A Church History of Scotland*, London: Oxford University Press, p. 418.
2 *Second Book of Discipline*, VII, 32, 40; see James Kirk edition, Edinburgh: Saint Andrew Press, 1980, pp. 205, 206.
3 Article 7.
4 See Chapter 1.
5 From a statement of the World Faith and Order Conference held at Lund, Sweden, in 1952.
6 Assembly Reports, 1962, p. 66.
7 Assembly Reports, 1962, p. 67.
8 Verbatim Record, General Assembly 1962, p. 7.
9 Assembly Reports, 1968, p. 522.
10 Verbatim Record, General Assembly, 1975, p. 275.
11 Verbatim Record, General Assembly, 1975, p. 276.
12 See Assembly Reports, 2000, pp. 1/9 and 1/35.
13 Assembly Reports, 2003, p. 27/4.

8

Changing Attitudes:
Inter-Faith Relations

RECENT DEVELOPMENTS

In 1993 the General Assembly received a report from the Board of World Mission and Unity entitled, 'Mission and Evangelism in a Multi-Faith Society and a Multi-Faith World'. The report explored the tension between the Church's traditional claims for the uniqueness of Christ with the call to mission in his name, and the cultural diversity found in contemporary Scotland and the wider world. After debating the report the Assembly remitted it to the Church for study. There was, however, an attempt in the Assembly to amend the seemingly innocuous deliverance of the Board which asked simply that, the report having been remitted for further study, the Working Party which had produced it should be thanked and discharged. The amendment, proposed by the Reverend Ian Hamilton, was in the following terms:

> The General Assembly re-state the Church of Scotland's commitment to the teaching of Scripture that Jesus Christ, the Son of God, incarnate, crucified and risen, is the only Saviour of men and women; and that through faith in him alone we become children of God; and re-affirm the Church of Scotland's commitment to world-wide evangelism.

While deploring intolerance and triumphalism, Mr Hamilton argued that the report was fatally flawed in that it 'failed to embrace the Church's divinely given missionary mandate'. 'It is not', he maintained, 'intolerant to proclaim Jesus Christ as the only mediator between God and man.'[1] The Convener, the Reverend Margaret Forrester, resisted the amendment. She explained that 'while being 99 per cent sympathetic' the 1 per cent was so important that, on theological, legal and practical grounds, she could not agree. Theologically, she argued that while 'we who confess Jesus Christ as Saviour and Lord stand within the new covenant of grace . . . God's grace is not to be limited by us'. Her legal argument was based on the 1879 Declaratory Act of the United Presbyterian Synod, quoted in the report, which the Procurator confirmed was one of the Leading Documents in the Basis and Plan of Union in 1929, thus forming an essential part of the constitution of the Church. This Act declared that it was not required to be held 'that God may not extend his grace to any without the pale of ordinary means, as may seem good in his sight'. To accept the addendum, Mrs Forrester argued, would mean 'a narrowing of the faith of the Church of Scotland as it has been expressed for over a hundred years'. Finally, the practical reason was that the whole point of the report was to stimulate discussion with people of other faiths. The effect of the addendum would be to 'close the door on the discussion before it had started'.[2] The Assembly agreed with the Convener by a sufficiently clear margin not to require a card vote. As a result seventy-nine commissioners entered their dissent. It was an interesting episode which illustrates the sensitivities surrounding this issue. For myself, I found, and still find most helpful, the report's references to a World Council of Churches' Conference held in 1989 at San Antonio, Texas, and in particular the statement, which has become known as the San Antonio Declaration: 'We cannot point to any other way of salvation than Jesus Christ; at the same time we cannot set limits to the saving power of God.'[3] Indeed, there are echoes here of the nineteenth-century Declaratory Acts on the Westminster Confession as they sought to affirm God's love and care for those beyond the reach of the gospel and reassure those deeply troubled by the doctrine of double predestination (see Chapter 10).

Reference was made in the previous chapter to the historic ecumenical address given by Archbishop Thomas Winning to the General Assembly of 1975. In 1984 something equally historic occurred when Mr Henry Tankel, FRCS, President of the United Synagogues of Scotland, became the first Jew to address the General Assembly. Earlier in the day the Assembly had received a Common Statement prepared by a joint consultation group set up two years previously, a statement which Mr Tankel described as representing 'a courage, vision and understanding, rare in this world'.[4] He spoke of 'a common belief in the one God, our mutual respect for human rights and dignity, our abhorrence of persecution and bigotry, our mutual desire for peace and our understanding of the importance of spiritual values in a material world'. The following year the Assembly received reports on Jewish–Christian Relations and on Anti-Semitism and was further informed of the possibility of engaging in similar consultations with the Muslim community. Over subsequent years inter-faith relations are mentioned increasingly in the report of the Committee on Ecumenical Relations. The 2000 report told how the Committee called a bi-annual meeting of representatives of different departments of the Church whose work was influenced by the multi-faith context. Reference was also made to the work of bodies such as the Churches' Agency for Inter-faith Relations and the Churches' Commission for Inter-faith Relations, the Board of National Mission's Well project in Pollokshields, the Glasgow Sharing of Faiths Group and an annual 'Meet Your Neighbour' event held in Glasgow's St Mungo Museum. The report went on to record the launch of the Scottish Inter-faith Council in October 1999, by Patricia Ferguson, MSP, Deputy Presiding Officer of the Scottish Parliament. The purpose of the Council, the report stated, was 'to enable the faith communities to work together on matters of mutual interest' and to 'provide a channel through which the faith communities can together address the Scottish Parliament'.

The election of the Scottish Parliament in 1999 focused attention on inter-faith matters in a very specific way. The question had arisen as to whether there should be prayers in the Parliament. Inevitably, there were differing views among politicians and religious communities. However, one thing upon which the politicians all appeared to be agreed was that, if there were to be prayers, then what happened in the House of Commons should not be the model. There, prayers follow the Anglican Prayer Book and are led by the Speaker's Chaplain who is a Canon of Westminster. The political view was that any Scottish pattern should be more diverse.

The issue became a topic of public debate. Some argued for exclusively Christian prayers; some even argued for a Church of Scotland (as national church) 'monopoly'; others favoured a multi-faith approach. In the event the Parliament opted for a weekly 'Time for Reflection' with slots allocated to the different faith groups on the basis of the number of their members and adherents. One MSP waggishly described this arrangement as 'proportional prayer' but, on the whole, it has worked well, affirming the place of religion in modern Scottish society and enabling a specific note of spiritual reflection to be sounded in the chamber.

However, what really brought inter-faith relations to the fore was 11 September 2001. Nobody will forget what they were doing that day, when they heard the terrible news from the United States, and the after-shocks of the catastrophe will remain for many years to come. One early casualty was inter-faith relations, with an almost immediate anti-Muslim backlash. In an unguarded moment President Bush described his 'war against terrorism' as a 'crusade', although, soon afterwards, he paid a very public visit to a mosque to affirm the 'Americanness' of American Muslims. In Scotland, within a few days of the atrocity, the Annandale Street Mosque in Edinburgh was fire-bombed. The following day the Moderator, the Right Reverend John Miller, paid a call on the Imam to express sympathy and solidarity, a visit which received much media coverage and was widely appreciated. The Moderator also encouraged ministers, when praying and reflecting with their congregations on world events, to seek opportunities of sharing with people of other faiths and, in the spring of 2002, he did just that himself when he accepted an invitation, extended to faith leaders world wide, to meet with the Pope in Assisi. Reference was made in the previous chapter to the first Scottish Ecumenical Assembly. This was held in Edinburgh in September 2001, shortly after 9/11, and several church leaders attending the gathering responded to an invitation from the Imam of the Potterrow Mosque across the road to share with members of the Muslim community in a time of quiet reflection. We sat quietly with our own thoughts and prayers and heard the Imam condemn the atrocity as not in any way pleasing to Islam.

A MODERATOR'S INTER-FAITH ENCOUNTERS

What follows now is largely anecdotal since inter-faith issues, partly by intention, but also simply in terms of responding to situations, became a significant theme of my own moderatorial year between May 2002 and May 2003.

During the summer of 2002 an invitation arrived for my wife and me to attend the annual Open Day and Tea Party at the Kagyu Samye Ling Monastery and Tibetan Centre at Eskdalemuir, Dumfriesshire. This community was established by Buddhist monks fleeing Chinese persecution in Tibet in the 1960s and has gained a wide following from people interested in meditation. Indeed, the friendly nun who greeted us told us that her mother was a Church of Scotland elder! At Samye Ling, along with other guests, we were warmly welcomed by the Abbot, the Venerable Lama Yeshe Losal, and I was invited to address some words of Christian greeting to the large, international gathering. Knowing that in the autumn I was to be visiting the predominantly Buddhist countries of Sri Lanka, Singapore and Burma it was helpful to have this contact and exposure.

In October and November of 2002 we travelled to south-east Asia. The lovely island of Sri Lanka had been ravaged by civil war for twenty years at a cost of some 65,000 lives. The root cause of the conflict was ethnic, with the minority Tamil Hindu population seeking independence from the majority Sinhalese Buddhist population. Caught in the crossfire was the Muslim community, which also had its own fears and aspirations. The National Council of Churches was much involved in the work of peace making and we were taken to see a number of church projects in the area around Trincomalee, in the north-east of the island. There, we saw at first hand the devastating consequences of civil war and the wretched plight of so many people, driven from their villages and their land. Of several projects which we visited one particularly stands out – a small Christian-run nursery school with pupils aged between three and five years drawn from the various ethnic groups – a small seed with great potential to yield a harvest of reconciliation. We met community leaders, military leaders, ceasefire monitors and religious leaders from the different faiths. All were agreed on the importance of people learning to live side by side, respecting difference and committed to peace.

The Moderator of the General Assembly is *ex officio* a President of the Council of Christians and Jews (CCJ), a body established in 1942 to promote dialogue and friendship between the two faiths. Other presidents include the Chief Rabbi and the Archbishop of Canterbury. In November 2002 the Queen gave a reception to mark the sixtieth anniversary of the founding of the CCJ, and I had the honour of presenting a number of distinguished guests to Her Majesty and the Duke of Edinburgh during the course of the event. I was also able to visit the offices of the Council during the Moderator's London visit and meet members of staff, both Christians and Jews working together in a common cause. January 2003 saw the national Holocaust Memorial event in Scotland, at Edinburgh's Usher Hall, where we were also included among the invited guests. The event was poignant in the extreme, reminding me of the two occasions on which I had visited the Yad Vashem Holocaust Memorial in Jerusalem.

On 11 September 2002 it had been arranged that I should preach at an anniversary service in Edinburgh's St Giles' Cathedral. Like the service held in the same place the previous year, immediately after the atrocity, it was both ecumenical and inter-faith in its approach. Dr Kenneth Collins of the Glasgow Jewish Representative Council read from the Old Testament and Councillor Bashir Maan, a prominent Muslim figure and author of *The New Scots: The Story of Asians in Scotland*, read verses from the Koran. The passage selected by Councillor Maan declared that what matters is not whether we pray to the east or to the west, but that our heart is pure and that we care for our kin and all in need. After the service a young American woman spoke to me at the door of the Cathedral. She said that, as a Christian, she had been very angry when she noticed from the Order of Service sheet that there was to be a reading from the Koran – but having heard the passage she was glad it had been included. As she put it, 'I didn't know there was stuff like that in the Koran.'

The following day, 12 September 2002, there was a gathering of faith leaders at Scottish Churches' House, Dunblane. The invitation to attend had gone out jointly from myself as Moderator, Archbishop Keith Patrick O'Brien (Roman Catholic Archbishop of Edinburgh and St Andrews and Chairman of the Bishops' Conference) and Bishop Bruce Cameron, Primus of the Scottish Episcopal Church. The spectrum covered Bahai, Buddhist, Christian, Hindu, Jew, Muslim and Sikh. The plan was to spend a day getting to know each other better, and each person had been asked to bring a symbol of their faith and speak of its significance. Such an inter-faith meeting was by no means novel, but what was new was the degree of involvement and energy being put in at a leadership level. The day attracted a fair amount of media coverage, much of it set within a 9/11 context and also the looming crisis over Iraq. I recall a long conversation with a Glasgow Imam who was vexed over the bullying and, in some cases, physical violence towards Muslim pupils in schools, the perpetrators, white pupils, viewing them as the enemy.

In January 2003 the group met again at the Glasgow Mosque with the same range of faiths present. Our homework had been to come prepared to say a few words about prayer in our own tradition and so we spoke and listened to one another. There was no argument about rights and wrongs of prayer – just a simple sharing, with some questions for further elucidation. After that we joined the congregation in the mosque for lunchtime prayers and in the afternoon had a discussion on the theme of peace. We concluded by agreeing a joint statement on the Iraq situation. One of the many interesting points for reflection during our morning discussion on prayer was the fact that the English word 'precarious' is derived from the Latin *precare*. We acknowledged our common tradition of prayer as we lived together in an increasingly precarious world.

In February the Moderator traditionally spends a couple of days in Brussels, meeting with Scottish MEPs and with representatives of the European Commission. Two of my recent predecessors, Sandy McDonald and John Cairns, had invited other Scottish church leaders to join them, but I felt the time was right to form a delegation which was both ecumenical and inter-faith in composition. In the event I led a party of twenty-one people, drawn from most of the Scottish Churches (including some, like the Free Church, the Associated Presbyterian Churches and the Baptist Church, not affiliated to ACTS) and the different faith communities. We were given presentations on themes such as immigration and asylum, the enlargement of the Community, the environment and the work of the Convention which, under the chairmanship of Valéry Giscard d'Estaing, was drafting a European constitution. As with all such events, the formal input was valuable, but the time together in conversation, sharing of meals and taxis, was also extremely useful in terms of building relationships. On our first evening we gathered in a Brussels restaurant which had been advised of our complex dietary requirements and was able to cope. After welcoming everyone I invited the group to keep silence for a few moments, so that each in his or her own way could give thanks for safe journeying, for the food prepared for us and ask a blessing on our time together. After the silence a member of the group said to me, 'I wondered how you would deal with that!'

Later in February my wife and I set off for the Middle East – a three-week visit which took us to Lebanon, Syria and Egypt. By this stage war in Iraq was looking increasingly inevitable, but, after some reflection and discussion, we decided that it was even more important that the visit should go ahead to demonstrate solidarity with our partner churches there.

The main focus of our time in Lebanon was a consultation involving our hosts, the Evangelical Synod of Syria and Lebanon and the Middle East Council of Churches, together with the Presbyterian Church in Ireland and the United Reformed Church. Our hosts were most anxious that we should speak about the opposition of the churches in the west to American and British policy in relation to Iraq and that this should be made more generally known within the wider community. So the Reverend John Waller (Moderator of the United Reformed Church) and I found ourselves addressing a large gathering in Beirut of Christian and Islamic leaders. We spoke of our Churches' concerns that proper place be given to the United Nations, that the weapons inspectors be given time and genuine opportunity, of our concerns for the ordinary people of Iraq, of the mistake in seeing what was unfolding as a conflict between Christian and Muslim and of the priority which should be given to a just resolution of the Israel–Palestine conflict, including the resolution of the refugee issue. Indeed, only the previous day we had visited the notorious Sabra camp. Our hosts were clearly very pleased with the meeting in that it underscored Christian–Muslim solidarity at a time when many Muslims were looking at their Christian neighbours with a degree of suspicion. I was particularly struck by the comment of a Sheik who spoke excellent English and thanked the Church of Scotland for the various statements on the Iraq crisis which had appeared on the Church's website.

Our journey into Syria provided a nice human and inter-faith moment. As we drove across the border from Lebanon we were told to leave our vehicle and were escorted to the office of the head of border security. We wondered what all this was about and were relieved to discover that the security chief, a Muslim, was a friend of the Moderator of the Synod who had told him to expect some important (his word, not mine) Presbyterian visitors from Scotland. So we were welcomed to Syria with sunflower tea and kindly greetings shared beneath a large photograph of President Assad.

As in Lebanon we sensed the growing tensions over Iraq and the concern of our Christian hosts that the position of the Churches in the west should be made known as widely as possible – not least among the majority Muslim population. So it was arranged that my time in Aleppo should include a meeting with the Great Mufti of Aleppo, Sheik Ahmed Badr-Din Hassoun. What was programmed as a half-hour conversation developed into a two-hour visit, concluding with a joint interview on Syrian television. The Mufti had a nice sense of humour. When reference was made to our common ancestor Abraham, his Muslim line of descent coming down through Hagar, my Judaeo–Christian line through Sarah, he remarked, 'your mother was the blonde, mine the brunette'. It was a cordial conversation, though he did get cross when I made reference to the fact that in Scotland Muslims were a minority within a predominantly Christian culture, whereas in Syria the opposite was the case. He insisted that this was not so, on the grounds that all Muslims are Christians as well. His argument was based on the fact that Muslims acknowledge

Jesus Christ as a great prophet and teacher. We talked around the topic for a bit, but it was clear he was not for shifting his ground.

Also in Syria, again arranged by the Evangelical Church, I met with the Grand Mufti of Syria, Sheik Ahmad Kuftaro. The Grand Mufti spoke of his 'uncle' Jesus Christ, greeted me as his 'cousin in faith' and invited me to bring a Christian greeting to the large congregation gathered in Damascus' Abu Nour Mosque for Friday prayers. I used the opportunity to stress the importance of Christian–Muslim dialogue and quoted from William Dalrymple's book, *From the Holy Mountain*,[5] in which he speaks of the centuries-long tradition of good Christian–Muslim relations in the Middle East – something from which the west can learn and, sadly, something, increasingly under threat. Indeed, in an article published in the *New York Times* in the summer of 2003 Dalrymple speaks of the Orthodox monastery of Saidnaya to the north of Damascus. 'On any given night', he writes, 'Muslim pilgrims far outnumber Christian ones . . . 'Ordinary Muslims', he continues, 'have not forgotten the line in the Koran about not disputing with the people of the book [that is Jews and Christians] save in the most courteous manner . . . and say we believe in what has been sent down to us and what has been sent down to you; our God and your God is one.'[6] Such 'pluralist equilibrium', as Dalrymple describes it, is now under threat by a new hardening of attitudes. Yet Dalrymple also quotes the Syrian Orthodox Metropolitan of Aleppo, 'Christians are better off in Syria than anywhere else in the Middle East.' 'Other than Lebanon', says the Patriarch, 'this is the only country in the region where a Christian can feel the equal of a Muslim.' This sentiment was reinforced in my own conversation with the Greek Orthodox Patriarch of Damascus, Ignatius IV, who, when I told him of my invitation to speak in the mosque, remarked that he 'loved the Grand Mufti as he loved his brother patriarchs'.

The final leg of our Middle East visit took us to Egypt – to Cairo, Luxor and Asiyut, the Upper Egypt heartland of the Presbyterian Church. Only in Asiyut did we feel any anxiety on the grounds of personal safety and that arose from the insistence of the local police on providing us with a guard for the duration of our visit. They also prevented us from visiting the grave of the Scottish missionary, John Hogg, on the grounds that it would take us into an area controlled by Muslim fundamentalists who had been behind recent attacks on churches. This was a reminder of real underlying tensions between the two faiths and the need for much work to be done to overcome them. We also learned of the difficulties and obstruction often experienced by churches in securing planning permission for building projects.

In Cairo the church authorities, like their colleagues in Lebanon and Syria, had also arranged for some inter-faith contact in the form of a meeting with Sheik Tantawy, the Grand Iman of Al-Ahzar, who in recent years has received visits from the Pope and the Archbishop of Canterbury, and who has established a serious unit on inter-faith dialogue. The day before our meeting with the Grand Imam the Al-Ahzar Council had issued a statement which characterised any war between the United States with the United Kingdom and Iraq as a conflict between Christian and Muslim and called for a *jihad* (a holy war) in response. We did our best to challenge this and explanations were offered to us, based on the strength of feeling and the regrettable use by President Bush of the word 'crusade'. At the same time the Grand Imam reiterated his commitment to Christian–Muslim dialogue.

It was, in many ways, a good time to be in the Middle East and to experience, no matter how briefly or superficially, something of Christian–Muslim relationships – particularly at such a tense and critical time. One afternoon, while being driven from Homs to Damascus, my mobile phone rang. It was a journalist from the *The Herald* newspaper wanting me to comment on something. 'Is it all right to talk?' he asked politely. 'You're not in the middle of anything?' Truthfully I replied: 'It's fine. Actually, I'm on the road to Damascus.' Indeed, it was something of a Damascus Road experience to view the world at such a time from the perspective of the Middle East.

Another story I like to tell is of an old man whom we met in Homs. He was the senior elder of the Presbyterian Church there and told us that, as a young engineer, he had spent a couple of years working on the hydro-electric scheme at Pitlochry. As a consequence, he had developed a life-long affection for Scotland. He also told us that he had a daughter, married to an Iraqi and living with her husband and children in Baghdad. Naturally, he was deeply worried for their safety, and we found ourselves thinking about them a great deal in the coming weeks. At the end of April 2003 I was in Canada, fulfilling a preaching engagement in the Church of St Andrew and St Paul, Montreal. At the end of the service a young Syrian woman came up to me. 'You met my uncle in Homs', she said. 'He told me all about your visit.' 'How is his family?' I asked. 'They're fine', was the welcome reply. A nice story about connections, but it also illustrates something deeper – the Middle East Christian diaspora. That young woman and her husband (also Syrian), like many other Christians from the region (Dalrymple estimates two million), are now making new lives for themselves in North America, Europe and Australia. King Hussein of Jordan once remarked: 'The Christians are the glue which holds the Middle East together. If they go the moderate Muslims will soon be driven out too.' The sad reality now is that many of them are going. The report of the Board of World Mission to the 2003 General Assembly makes a similar point when it speaks of the role of Churches in the region 'to mediate and to stand for truth and justice'. Reference is also made to a statement by the Rabbis for Human Rights in Israel: 'In defending ourselves we must always hold on to the prophetic vision of decency and humanity.' To illustrate such decency and humanity, transcending the ethnic and religious divide, the report goes on to recall the moving story of nineteen-year-old Yoni Jesner, a Jew from Glasgow, who was killed in a suicide bomb attack in Israel, and whose family donated his kidney to save the life of a young Palestinian girl, Yasmin Ramila.

After returning from the Middle East I had opportunities of sharing something of the experience, not only within the Church, but also with the wider community, including Muslim friends. There is a clear commitment by the Scottish Executive and Parliament to eliminate sectarianism and, in commending this initiative in a sermon preached at the Kirking of the Scottish Parliament in May 2003, I made the point that we need to move to break down the barriers of suspicion and distrust, not just between Catholic and Protestant, but across the whole religious and cultural spectrum. At the General Assembly the outgoing Moderator is given a slot to report on his or her year. In 2003 I took the opportunity of talking about some of my inter-faith contacts and was delighted when a group of individuals with whom I have become involved from the different faith communities accepted my invitation to be present when I gave my report. They were deeply touched by the warmth of the applause when the Moderator, Professor Torrance, invited them to stand and be recognised.

In June 2003 I was an invited guest, along with Archbishop Mario Conti of Glasgow, at a ceremony at the Glasgow Central Mosque when Prince Charles opened the new Islamic cultural and community centre. On my arrival at Glasgow's Queen Street station I got into a taxi. I was dressed in a clerical shirt and collar. 'Where to?' enquired the cabbie. 'The Mosque', I replied. He was on the point of moving off, when he put the gear stick into neutral, applied the handbrake and turned round. That's not what I was expecting you to say!' he remarked. I replied, 'Times are changing.'

I hope they are and certainly, it did seem to me, at the very least, that a Christian response to Iraq must involve a commitment to dialogue and interaction with people of faith. I was once asked what the outcome of such dialogue and interaction might be and I don't find that a particularly easy question to answer beyond what might sound platitudinous – greater understanding and a society and a world more at ease with itself. Clearly there are issues of profound disagreement between the faiths – not only theologically, but also socially – from the role of women to the ritual slaughter of animals. But then fairly deep disagreements exist within the Church family too.

In August 2003 what was becoming known as 'the faith leaders' group' met again on Holy Island, off Arran. As at the Glasgow Mosque in January, and at Dunblane the previous September, there was a good representation of faiths present on this ancient place of pilgrimage. Holy Island, reached by the small ferry from Lamlash, is now home to a Buddhist community. A house at the south end of the island provides the perfect location for those engaging in three-year retreats. However, we were just there for the day and our visit was based on the new Centre close by the pier. The Centre is surrounded by a lovely garden which our host, Lama Yeshe Losal, proudly showed us before leading us off to visit the cave which had been the hermitage home of the seventh-century Christian monk, Molaise. Lama Yeshe pointed out the ancient Celtic cross carved into the rock above the cave entrance. We continued our walk and soon came to some more recent religious decoration in the form of colourful Buddhist rock paintings. We fell into a discussion on symbols and the ways in which they represent the mysteries of faith which are often difficult to express. The pluralism of the group was apparent when one of our number, a Buddhist sister, who had been brought up in the Church of Scotland (the one whose mother is a Kirk elder), turned to me and said: 'It's like the hymn we sang in Sunday School – number 12 in the hymn book – "Immortal, Invisible, God only wise, in light inaccessible, hid from our eyes".[7] This Holy Island gathering had its own distinctive quality arising from the sheer fact that we travelled together on the Arran Ferry, crossed to Holy Island itself in the small open ferry boat, walked and talked in groups around the island and shared a wonderful vegetarian meal. It felt more like friends having a day out than a formal religious meeting and further strengthened the personal ties which linked us in this journey of sharing faith. We departed having arranged our next gathering in March 2004 which was held at the Glasgow New Synagogue.

Clearly, as Christians we have our Lord's command to go and make disciples of all nations, which brings us back to the controversy in the 1993 General Assembly over the question of inter-faith dialogue. There are Christians who believe that the only appropriate dialogue with people of other faiths is one which has conversion to Christianity as its objective. Indeed, when in the immediate aftermath of 9/11 my moderatorial predecessor wrote to all ministers encouraging them to seek to build bridges with the Muslim community, and perhaps to meet with Muslims for reflection and prayer, he received critical letters from some who thought this was undermining the unique saving message of the gospel. We come back to San Antonio: 'As Christians we can point to no other salvation than that which is in Jesus Christ; at the same time we can never presume to set limits to the saving power of God.'

In 2002 the Chief Rabbi, Jonathan Sacks, had a book published entitled *The Dignity of Difference*. I leave the last word to him:

We will make peace only when we learn that God loves difference and so, at last, must we. God has created many cultures, civilisations and faiths, but only one world in which to live together – and it is getting smaller all the time.[8]

NOTES

1 Verbatim Record, General Assembly, 1983, pp. 661–5.
2 Verbatim Record, General Assembly, 1983, pp. 675–7.
3 Assembly Reports, 1993, p. 581.
4 Verbatim Record, General Assembly, 1984, p. 614.
5 See William Dalrymple, *From the Holy Mountain*, London: HarperCollins, 1997, pp. 185–91.
6 *New York Times*, 7 June 2003.
7 The reference is to the *Revised Church Hymnary*.
8 Jonathan Sacks, *The Dignity of Difference*, London: Continuum, 2002, p. 23.

9

Changing Attitudes: Human Sexuality

CHANGING ATTITUDES

One of the most divisive issues facing the Church at the present time is human sexuality. The debate has become especially strident over attitudes towards homosexuality, particularly, though not exclusively, in relation to the clergy.

Social attitudes towards sex have changed dramatically over the past fifty years. We have come a long way from the criminalisation of homosexual activity between consenting adult males in private to today's 'gay pride' movement. For example, it would have been impossible for cabinet ministers to be openly homosexual in the 1950s. Attitudes towards heterosexual relations have also changed. Nowadays the phrase 'living in sin' has a decidedly old-fashioned ring to it. Fifty years ago it was not considered at all 'respectable' for a couple to live together before they were married. Now it is almost becoming the norm, partly on the basis of seeing how things work out before the commitment of marriage, and partly on economic, cost-sharing grounds. Indeed, heterosexual co-habitation is for many a chosen long-term option in preference to marriage. The term 'partner' has increasingly common currency, rather than 'husband' or 'wife'. The further question has arisen as to whether those who choose partnership rather than marriage should be accorded the same legal rights as married people, including those who live in same-sex partnerships. In June 2003 the Department of Trade and Industry issued a consultation document entitled, 'Civil Partnership: A Framework for the Legal Recognition of Same-sex Couples', and in a foreword Minister of State, Jacqui Smith, MP, explained the rationale by referring to distress caused to partners of seriously ill patients refused hospital visits which would automatically be granted to a husband or wife. Other examples include pension rights, or the right to stay in a shared home after one partner dies.

Such questions are clearly testing ones for the Church, which has traditionally held that the only legitimate context for sexual activity is life-long marriage between a man and a woman. In days when the Church was socially powerful this teaching was ruthlessly enforced, with fornicators hauled before the Kirk Session, or made to endure the rebuking stool before the whole congregation. An Act of the General Assembly of 1648 'For the Remedies of the grievous and common sins of the Land in this present time' established elders' districts with the requirement that the elder 'visit the same every month at least, and report to the Session what scandals and abuses are therein'. (I wonder how that would go down today!) Those who had 'fallen into fornication' were to make 'publick profession of repentance three severall Sabbaths'. In the case of a second offence this increased to six sabbaths, rising to twenty-six sabbaths for a third relapse. Horror stories are told of girls concealing their pregnancies and killing their babies at birth, rather than face disgrace and punishment. In later centuries young, unmarried pregnant women would be sent away and 'cared for' in institutions for 'bad girls', with their children taken from them at birth. Inevitably, given the values of the time, values supported by the Church, the female 'fornicator' invariably suffered to a far greater degree than her male partner.

The Church no longer has such power to enforce the rule of fidelity or celibacy and is having to come to terms with the reality of the sexual revolution which has taken place since the middle of the twentieth century. Increasingly, couples seeking Christian marriage are already living together. Some ministers 'give them a hard time' and even insist on a period of living apart before the wedding. Others take the view that it is good that they are 'doing the right thing' and, in a welcoming way, encourage them towards the commitment of Christian marriage. There have been cases, too, of same-sex couples coming to seek the Church's blessing on their relationship, though, given the Church's traditional view of homosexuality, there have not been many. In the General Assembly of 1993 the attention of the Assembly was drawn to such a ceremony of blessing and an attempt made to forbid such a thing from ever happening again. A commissioner moved: 'In view of the recent publicity given to a Kirk minister's Service of Blessing on a "marriage" of two lesbians, instruct all Church of Scotland ministers not to perform services of blessing on homosexual/lesbian relationships'. At the time I was Depute Clerk to the Assembly and intervened in the debate to counsel against issuing such a sweeping instruction on one pastoral matter among many. I argued that the Church had a long tradition of trusting its ministers to make appropriate judgements in pastoral situations and that we should not be making *ad hoc* exceptions without some kind of considered process. The Assembly agreed and the motion was defeated, though both strength of feeling and division of opinion were evident in the voting figures of 338 for the motion and 534 against. For the avoidance of doubt, the Assembly did go on to make clear that, should the question arise again, there was no special service for such ceremonies.

The Debate in the 1950s and 1960s

The report of the Church and Nation Committee to the General Assembly of 1955 contained a short paragraph headed 'Homosexuality'. This read as follows:

> The attention of the Committee has been drawn to the setting up by the Home Secretary and the Secretary of State for Scotland of a Committee to examine the Law of Homosexuality and Prostitution [the Wolfenden Committee]. Certain evidence indicating the problem to be more extensive than had appeared at the outset has been brought to the notice of the [Church and Nation] Committee, leading it to arrange for a more intensive study. The question of giving evidence to the official Committee will be considered carefully and such steps taken as may be found will best express the views of the Church.[1]

The following year the Committee reported more fully on 'the problem' and confirmed that there was 'convincing evidence that indulgence in homosexual practices [was] much more prevalent in

Scotland than [had] been generally realised'.[2] The Committee went on to distinguish between orientation and practice, observing that

> there are many men and women with homosexual tendencies who live admirable lives of service to the community and to the Church, whose condition is unsuspected by those with whom they come in contact, and who never indulge in criminal sexual conduct. Such people are entitled to unqualified sympathy and respect. There are, however, other homosexuals who give expression to their nature by physical acts. In fairness, it must be recognised that the homosexual is subject to difficulties which the normal individual of heterosexual disposition escapes. For the true homosexual there can be no prospect of a satisfactory marital relationship, and the conventional segregation of the sexes in modern society, which helps to preserve the morality of the rest of the community, is to the homosexual often an added source of temptation.

Such recognition notwithstanding, the Committee concluded that 'from the Christian standpoint indulgence in homosexual practices is a sin from which the individual must be dissuaded and redeemed'.[3]

The Committee went on to consider the case for a change in the law which would decriminalise homosexual acts between consenting adults in private. It acknowledged that the current position led to such evils as blackmail, reluctance to seek help for fear of self-incrimination, inconsistency in applying the law and risk to young people through a preference for young partners 'less likely to demand large sums as the price of silence'. Nevertheless, the Committee, while welcoming the enquiry being conducted by the Wolfenden Committee, and giving an undertaking to study its recommendations, felt unable to express 'any firm opinion on the probable social effect of a relaxation of the criminal law'.[4]

In 1958 the Church and Nation Committee reported on the conclusions of Wolfenden, the 'most controversial' of which was the recommendation that homosexual acts, committed in private between consenting males above the age of twenty-one, should be removed from the realm of the criminal law. This proposal had been supported by all members of the Wolfenden Committee, with one exception, a Mr James Adair, who was, interestingly, also a commissioner from the Presbytery of Glasgow to that year's General Assembly. Mr Adair's concern was that the proposal would be regarded as 'condoning or licensing licentiousness and [would] open up for such people a new field of permitted conduct with unwholesome and distasteful implications'. The Church and Nation Committee noted that Christian opinion was divided 'between those who share Mr Adair's misgivings and those who would accept the reasoning and the conclusions of a majority of members of the Wolfenden Committee'.[5] Indeed, the Church and Nation Committee had itself been deeply divided. A sub-committee, which had been examining the matter for two years, had, in fact, come to the conclusion that Wolfenden was correct. However, this view had not been accepted by the main Committee which recommended that the General Assembly should regard such legal changes 'as inopportune, as liable to serious misunderstanding and misinterpretation, and as calculated to increase, rather than diminish this grave evil'. A Petition was presented to the Assembly on behalf of the sub-committee which had failed to persuade the Church and Nation Committee to adopt its view. This led to a counter-motion asking that Wolfenden be welcomed as 'a fair minded exposition' and that its principal recommendation be supported. The counter-motion also called on the Assembly to emphasise that 'all homosexual acts are sinful as breaches of Divine Law and must incur the condemnation of Christian conscience and the Christian Church'.[6] In the vote the recommendation of the Committee prevailed over the counter-motion and the Church of Scotland became the only major Church to oppose the Wolfenden Committee's proposal to amend the law.[7]

Homosexuality next came before the General Assembly in 1967, responsibility for the topic having passed in the interim from the Church and Nation Committee to the Moral Welfare Committee. The previous year the General Assembly had been persuaded that the matter should be looked at again. The tone of this report was strongly pastoral and, notwithstanding the clearly expressed view of the Assembly in 1958 that legal sanctions should continue to apply, the Committee, somewhat paradoxically (if not recklessly), described as 'satisfactory' the fact 'that the strict law, with regard to private homosexual acts between consenting adults in private, [was] no longer being enforced'.[8] Psychological factors were also adduced to explain homosexuality – 'broken homes, an over-possessive mother, or any departure from normal, happy family life'. The theological doctrines of forgiveness and redemption were also strongly emphasised and the report concluded by warning of the dangers of so isolating homosexuals that it would become difficult 'for the Church to approach them in order to try to win them from their sinful ways and redeem them from their wrong desires'.[9] The recommendations arising from the report asked that the General Assembly call for

> a more sympathetic understanding of the difficulties and handicaps of those suffering from homosexual tendencies . . . regret the comparative lack of psychiatric and medical treatment available . . . and that ministers [should] show special pastoral concern and care to those suffering from such tendencies, so that they may know that the Gospel of redemption through Jesus Christ is for all.

The Committee also called for the Assembly to support the decriminalisation of homosexual acts between consenting adults in private.

These proposals were roundly rejected and, in place of them, the Assembly 'deplored the prevalence of homosexual practices as a source of uncleanness and deterioration in human character and of weakness and decadence in the nation's life'. At the same time the Assembly 'being deeply concerned for the souls of all who are subject to homosexual temptations, [urged] them to believe that there is salvation and freedom for them in Jesus Christ . . .'

The following year the Committee was blunt with the General Assembly and stated 'its considered opinion that last year's deliverance has proved unhelpful'.[10] To justify this opinion the Committee explained that, when the 1967 report was made public prior to the Assembly, homosexual men 'began seeking help and counsel' from church agencies. The report continued:

> not one single man has come . . . seeking help since 24th May, 1967, the day the Committee's proposed deliverance was rejected; those who had been coming never came back, and no fresh ones have ever appeared; thus any work of rehabilitation or pastoral care has ceased. Some who have such homosexual tendencies have stated despairingly that they now consider that the Church's attitude is one of unfeeling condemnation.[11]

The Committee pleaded with the General Assembly to adopt a more compassionate approach and to support the deliverance which had been presented the year before. This time the Committee's plea was successful.

The Debate in the 1980s and 1990s

It was 1983 before the General Assembly again considered the issue of homosexuality. Two years previously the Board of Social Responsibility had set up a study group to consider the 1968 position in the light of continuing debate within the wider Church and community. Like previous reports this latest one looked at Biblical texts, questions of human formation and sexual orientation, common misconceptions (for example, that homosexuality is a form of paedophilia) and the Church's pastoral response. The report recognised that there were differing interpretations of those Biblical texts considered relevant. It also acknowledged, with sadness, that

> it is not unusual for homosexual people, who have little opportunity for fellowship within the Church, to rely instead on the support and understanding which they find in Gay Groups which have no sympathy with the life-giving message of the Gospel.[12]

At the same time, the Board made clear its view that 'the practice of homosexual acts is not the way God would have his people live'. There was an acknowledgement that 'some Christian homosexuals will see in an active homosexual partnership a love which is in no way contrary to that described by Christ in his life and witness'. However, there would be 'others, vexed by tensions within themselves which they would wish to disown [who would be] made profoundly aware of their frail humanity and their need for help'. Faced with these two outlooks, the Church's response was 'to point the way to a greater love, transcending the sexual, towards which [both] may be drawn'.[13] Finally, the report concluded with strong words of support for homosexual people, describing them as 'a group that has suffered more than its share of oppression and contempt' and so 'has a particular claim upon the concern of the Church'.[14] The proposed deliverance asked the Assembly to receive the report and commend it as a guide to all who have to cope with homosexuality, and this was duly approved.

The next time these questions came to the General Assembly was in 1994. That year the Panel on Doctrine brought forward a report on the theology of marriage and the Board of Social Responsibility presented a further report on human sexuality.

The Panel's report offered a scholarly reflection on marriage in Scripture and in Christian tradition, building on work done in a previous study in the 1950s when the Church moved (in 1959) to permit the remarriage of divorced persons in Church. At the same time the Panel engaged, as the Church had a right to expect, with changing perceptions of marriage and other relationships in contemporary society. Reflecting on the modern situation the Panel observed:

> One possible response by the Church to these rapidly changing social patterns would be to lament the dwindling influence of the Church within the community, and to interpret the changes as evidence of a lurch away from Christian standards and family values, towards irresponsibility and moral chaos. We believe that such a response would be simplistic and misleading, since it fails to take account of those committed Christians who choose, quite deliberately and in good faith, patterns of relationship other than traditional marriage.

The Panel warned:

> The Church ... is facing a new situation. It can no longer be assumed that those who enter into relationships other than marriage, even *Christians* who enter into such relationships, will accept the traditional evaluation of their lifestyle as deviant, morally wrong, or a matter for contrition, repentance and change. It seems to us undeniable that a huge gulf has opened up between the Church's traditional teaching and the views of many younger church members. It is a gulf which perhaps extends beyond the young; many parents feel respect, rather than censure, for life choices made by their children which are different from the choices they themselves made.[15]

The report recognised that there were differing views within the Church, with some considering the appropriate response to be an adherence to traditional teaching, while others sought to interpret the faith in ways which recognised that absolute categories of right and wrong were not helpful in dealing with such complex realities. It was noted that the Church of England, in a House of Bishop's Statement of

1991, had declared that there was place within the Christian fellowship for a 'loving and faithful homophile partnership' (though for clergy of homosexual orientation celibacy was the norm) and that the American Episcopalian Church had ordained self-avowed practising homosexual persons to the priesthood. And, in a section of the report, dealing specifically with same-sex relationships, the Panel urged tolerance and mutual respect for different views:

> Those whose faith encompasses the possibility of God's involvement in same-sex relationships have no right to require the same perspective from those who believe as a matter of conscience that homosexuals should live in perpetual celibacy. Those who regard all homosexual relationships as intrinsically evil have, equally, no right to impose their view on others, who perceive in some same-sex partnerships qualities of which they sincerely believe God approves.[16]

Based on its analysis, the Panel asked the Assembly to reaffirm marriage 'as one of God's great gifts to humanity for the well being of husband and wife, the security of growing children and the social health of the community'. At the same time a word of caution was entered over the use of the term 'family values', 'which can be used as a slogan to hurt or alienate those who are not part of a nuclear family'. The Assembly was also asked to 'recognise that Christians in good faith hold diverse interpretations of God's will in the area of sexual ethics', 'to affirm celibacy as a valid Christian life-choice' and to 'affirm love, trust, forgiveness and faithfulness as the most significant criteria by which all relationships are to be assessed; and [to] urge congregations not to discriminate against any person on grounds of marital status or sexual orientation'.[17]

This was radical stuff indeed, going well beyond anything contained in previous reports. While, in the past, as we have seen, there had been many expressions of pastoral concern for homosexual people, the perspective had invariably been that the condition was 'a problem' and that, while the Church recognised that it should love the sinner, there was no denying that indulgence in homosexual practices was a sin. Now, the Panel on Doctrine was suggesting that, instead of supporting the homosexual in the struggle towards celibacy, or even seeking a 'cure' for his or her 'disability', the Church should actually affirm and accept who and what they were. It was not surprising therefore that the Panel itself was split (the report was approved by eight votes to six) and, indeed, the six opposing members dissented from this section of the report. The dissent, published with the report, acknowledged that the issues raised and conclusions reached 'will inevitably expose deep divisions within the Church'. Nine grounds of dissent were listed, including a concern that the report failed sufficiently to represent the traditional view of marriage, that it implied a moral equivalence between marriage on the one hand and same-sex or pre-marital relationships on the other, and that it placed too much importance on acceptance of people as they are as distinct from urging them to seek radical renewal and transformation through God's grace.

As noted above, the General Assembly of 1994 also received a report from the Board of Social Responsibility, specifically on the subject of human sexuality. This was a substantial document, arising out of a debate in 1992 on family matters and covering themes such as the development of personhood, sexuality and people with mental and physical disability, sexuality and elderly people, as well as the issue of homosexuality. The Board referred to the debate over whether sexual orientation was genetically given, or socially acquired, a debate which it considered inconclusive. It recognised the diversity of opinion, not only on that question but on other matters such as Biblical interpretation. One area, however, in which the Board allowed no room for argument was over the social prejudice endured by homosexuals who were so often the target of insensitive and hurtful jokes. 'Many "liberals" and "conservatives" alike', the Board opined, 'are united in calling for respect for members of the homosexual minority and in condemning any kind of stigmatisation'.

The Board's conclusion was

> that for many in the Church of Scotland, their view about homosexuality would still be the one outlined in the 1983 report. Questions about causation, alternative interpretations of Scripture, and cultural factors are not enough to alter that view. At the same time, the Board would also recognise that in the Church of Scotland there are some who are convinced that in light of scientific evidence, socio-psychological understanding, critical scholarship and personal testimony, the view of homosexual practice as necessarily sinful can no longer be held with integrity and sincerity.

Having considered all the issues in light of the contemporary situation, the Board asked the General Assembly to commend the report to the Church:

- to facilitate informed discussion and understanding of the issues involved;

- to recognise that sexuality is a blessing and gift from God to be experienced and enjoyed without shame or guilt; and marriage is appointed as the right and proper setting for the full expression of physical love between man and woman;

- to note the presence of differing views, but see no compelling reasons to alter the Church's position that the practice of homo- sexual acts is contrary to God's will for humankind;

- and to deplore all prejudice against and maltreatment of people because of their sexual orientation and urge all congregations to welcome with Christian love and care all who are struggling with problems relating to their sexuality.

Faced with these two reports, both dealing with questions in the area of human sexuality, but saying rather different things, the Assembly's Business Committee developed a methodology for dealing with them both in the course of one debate. However, the Assembly itself had different ideas and preferred a proposal from the floor that the issues should most certainly be debated, but that no votes on issues of substance should be taken. This meant that the deliverances (recommendations) attached to the reports would not be put to the Assembly. Those who advocated this approach argued that it was quite apparent that the Church was deeply divided on the matter, that feelings were running high and that little would be gained (indeed much would be lost) were things to be pushed to a point of winners and losers. It was certainly important that the Assembly engage with the matters raised in both reports, but beyond that it was not helpful to go. This way of proceeding was itself the subject of an intense debate under the report of the Business Committee. Some felt that the Assembly should take a clear decision that could then be articulated as the position of the Church of Scotland. Others felt that the price of taking such a decision would be too high in terms of aggrieved and alienated members, both of the Assembly and the wider Church. In the event, the Assembly decided to adopt the procedure advocated. When it came to the debate, the two reports would be taken together, but no decisions of substance on the merits would be taken. A point of order was raised. Did a decision to adopt this procedure require a two-thirds majority as a suspension of Standing Orders? The Principal Clerk advised and the Moderator ruled that it did not. Points of order also featured in the debate itself, when it came three days later. Did the fact that the General Assembly was deliberately not taking a view on homosexuality mean that the previous deliverance of 1983 remained the position of the Church? The debate, while containing many well-argued and passionate speeches, was not a particularly edifying affair, serving largely to highlight the strength of feeling on both sides of the argument and the depth of disagreement within the Church.

At the end of the day, in the case of the Panel on Doctrine's report, the Assembly instructed the Panel, in consultation with the Board of Parish Education, to prepare guidelines for congregational study of the issues raised. The Social Responsibility Report was simply commended to the Church to facilitate informed discussion and understanding of the issues involved. In due course guidelines were produced which included role-play scenarios in which the daughter of a respected and traditional elder tells her parents that she is moving in with her boyfriend – hardly an exceptional circumstance today. Variations on a theme developed equivalent same-sex possibilities. I have a memory of using this material in my own Kirk Session at the time and finding it not particularly easy. Some elders, indeed, expressed their unhappiness at the use of such materials at all, while others acknowledged that the situations outlined reflected the reality of the world in which the contemporary Church was set.

On the issue of homosexuality the 1994 General Assembly was a bit like the Battle of Sheriffmuir. 'Some said that we'd won, and some said that they'd won, and some said that nane won at a' man!' The Panel on Doctrine which had sought to move the Assembly to a position of acceptance of same-sex relationships could say that the Assembly had not rejected its thinking, nor endorsed the views of the Board of Social Responsibility. Conversely, the Board could argue that its assertion of the 'traditional' view had not been repudiated, while the Panel's radical thinking had not been affirmed. Undeniably, many would have preferred a clearer signal so that the Church could express an unequivocal view. Equally, there were many who were grateful for the breathing space to debate the issues and the implicit recognition that the principle of liberty of opinion was being brought into play in the area of sexual ethics.

The Section 28 Controversy

Five years later the Church, once again, found itself embroiled in controversy over homosexuality. In 1999 the new Scottish Parliament began its work and one of the early priorities of the Executive was to remove from the statute book a piece of legislation, introduced by the Westminster Parliament in 1986 (Section 28 of the Local Government Act) designed to prevent materials promoting homosexuality from being used in schools, and to stop councils funding educational material which overtly promoted homosexual practice. In Scotland the measure was incorporated in Section 2A of the Local Government Act. Those promoting the amendment expressed a concern that the clause may have acted as a constraint upon teachers who were unsure precisely what they were permitted to teach. They felt that the existence of the measure contributed to a general climate of homophobia in society and urged that sex education should be as fully informed as possible. Those opposing repeal did not accept that the existence of the clause prevented genuine discussion of homosexuality as an orientation and considered that repeal would, effectively, undermine marriage, family life and the norm of heterosexuality. Within a very short time the whole nation seemed to be engulfed in controversy. A powerful alliance of Roman Catholic and Protestant Evangelicals, led by the late Cardinal Winning (who described homosexuality as 'a perversion') and Mr Brian Soutar, campaigned fiercely to retain the legislation, fearing that its abolition would lead to the active promotion of homosexuality in schools. The Kirk's Board of Social Responsibility aligned itself with this campaign. Meantime, many educationalists supported the move to abolish Section 28 on the grounds that what was envisaged was most certainly not promotion of any particular life style, but the imparting of knowledge and understanding to young people in an area of great emotional complexity. The Kirk's Committee on Education aligned itself with this point of view, as did the Moderator of the day, the Right Reverend John Cairns. A consequence of this was that the Church of Scotland spoke not with one voice, but two, something which many found disturbing, though others found it refreshing, liberating, healthy and honest.

As the General Assembly of 2000 approached it was clear that Section 28 would be on the agenda. However, mindful of 1994, rather than having two reports saying different things, it was generally agreed that it would be helpful were the Board of Social Responsibility and the Committee on Education to prepare and present a joint report. Representatives of both bodies, mindful that their differing opinions arose from a common commitment to the gospel, met and together produced a report. This was largely adopted by the Assembly, though not without debate. For example, the report, in the second section of its proposed deliverance, asked simply that the Assembly reaffirm the foundational nature of marriage. Two amendments were proposed. The first of these sought to add the words: 'as the God-given, accepted and proven building block of society'. This was rejected, some arguing that it undermined and devalued the place of single people in society. A second amendment sought to add the words: 'and that love is the most important aspect of any relationship', but this also was rejected. However, a counter-motion narrowly carried (by 336 votes to 329) and this became the finding of the Assembly. It declared: 'The General Assembly adheres to its previous decisions that affirm marriage as the normative context for heterosexual, permanent relationships and, by extension, as the appropriate environment in which to raise and nurture children.' The Assembly also called on the Scottish Executive, in a proposed replacement of Section 2A, to require Councils 'in the performance of those of its functions which relate principally to children, to have a regard to the value of marriage, parental commitment and family relationships in a child's development'. It further urged the Executive 'to fund in-service training so that teaching staff are well equipped to provide good sex education' and 'to promote new legislation addressing the issue of external monitoring of local government funding given to those groups whose remit concerns sexual health and sexual behaviour'.

Prior to the debate two notices of motion had been given. One welcomed the proposed repeal while the other urged the Scottish Executive to retain the clause. These two 'head-on' motions would certainly have created the 'fight-to-the-finish' debate which the 1994 Assembly declined to allow. The 2000 Assembly exercised similar caution with the Church's unity and peace and approved a proposal from the immediate past moderator, the Very Reverend John Cairns, not to debate these motions but simply to unite around what had been agreed. The following day *The Herald* newspaper, in a scathing editorial, declared: 'The Church of Scotland would like to claim a place in the centre of Scottish life. We believe it should do so, but on the evidence of yesterday's craven performance on Section 28, the Kirk has abrogated that right.' The article accused the Church of setting more value on its unity than on offering comment on 'an issue of great moral, spiritual and social importance'.[18] This was far from fair. The General Assembly, as we have seen, did debate the matter and offered some forthright and constructive comment. Clearly, the media were hoping for a bitter and divisive debate and were annoyed when the Assembly failed to oblige.

It cannot be denied, however, that while the 1994 Assembly encouraged a wider debate within the Church, there has been a definite reluctance to engage with the issue. The love that dare not speak its name has become the subject that dare not raise its head. Such reticence is owing mainly to a recognition of how divisive the matter has been for churches around the world. The Church of Scotland has had a painful history of division over such diverse matters as the Burgess Oath, the old and new light controversies, the right of a congregation to call its own minister, the relationship between Church and State and the status of the Westminster Confession of Faith. Was a person's attitude to homosexuality now to be declared a fundamental doctrine of the faith, dividing congregations and, perhaps, even families and leading, potentially, to schism, litigation and a fight to the finish for the name and title of the Church of Scotland? I recall one among many letters sent to the Moderator at the height of the 1999–2000 Section 28 controversy. The author, who signed himself 'Yours in Christ', stated simply that he deplored the Moderator's recent call for a rational debate on the matter. Writing in *The Herald* on 3 July 2003 Ron Ferguson quoted Reynolds Price, Professor of English literature at Duke University, North Carolina, on the subject: 'Many self-labelled Christians outclass the spitting cobra in the quantity and rage of their hurled venom.'[19] The fact is that to date the Church has not found it easy to have a rational debate and many are, therefore, nervous about starting any debate at all. There is also a view that there are more important matters for the Church to discuss. The Joint Report of the Board of Social Responsibility and the Education Committee, referred to above, stated with some exasperation: 'we regret that in a society faced with so many important moral issues which should be the concern of all Christians, so much time and energy has been devoted to this one issue'.[20]

Into the Twenty-first Century

In the summer of 2003, the Church of England appeared poised to appoint its first gay bishop in the person of Canon Jeffrey John. Professionally Canon John was qualified in every way for consecration as Bishop of Reading and made no secret of his sexual orientation. While he had not always been celibate and, indeed, had a long-term partner, he announced that he had been celibate for many years and would continue to be so. His nomination was a source of great controversy within the Church of England and the wider Anglican Communion, particularly in countries such as Nigeria, where Christianity is in 'fierce competition' with Islam – itself strongly opposed to homosexuality. Eventually Canon John withdrew. Meantime, in the United States, the Episcopal Church proceeded to appoint Canon Gene Robinson as Bishop of New Hampshire, a previously married man now with a same-sex partner, who was not celibate and whose nomination had been approved democratically in accordance with the Church's procedures.

It was inevitable that the Church of Scotland would be asked to comment on these proceedings, and it did so, initially through an interview given to the *Sunday Times*[21] by the Moderator, Professor Iain Torrance, on the proposed appointment of Canon Jeffrey John. Mindful of the fact that Canon John had been celibate for many years, Professor Torrance commented that he would be 'utterly untroubled' by the election of homosexual ministers as long as they were 'disciplined' and 'effective'. The Moderator's views were reported on the front page under a banner headline, 'Moderator backs gay ministers'. The article went on to quote a minister as being 'appalled' and 'troubled' by these comments, though two weeks later the same newspaper reported the result of a telephone poll of 200 ministers that it had conducted. This revealed that 76 (38 per cent) said 'they did not agree that gays had any place in ministry' while 'the remainder said they would be relaxed about the appointment of a homosexual minister'.[22]

Certainly Professor Torrance's comments reawakened controversy over the issue of homosexuality, particularly in relation to ministers. At the very least, clarification was sought as to what he meant, including a prominently featured open letter to the *Scotsman*.[23] In his response the Moderator made clear that he was talking about the person 'of self-disclosed orientation who lives a chaste and disciplined life'. He went on:

> There is a world of difference between an open homosexual in the sense of someone who is graciously allowed by society and the church to say, 'This is how I am. I have different awareness and gifts and I put them at the service of God and the Church' and someone who is open in the sense of engaging in practice.

He described his argument as:

> simple and theological, namely: 'Did Jesus Christ not die and rise again for all of us? Did he not die for gay people? May they not be baptised? And if baptised, and qualified by the requisite gifts and learning, may they not be ordained? Or do they have some deficiency in their humanity which is so irremediable that they are beyond the scope of the incarnation?'[24]

Those who expressed themselves as 'troubled' by the original *Sunday Times* article were reassured by the clarification that the Moderator was talking about orientation only, and not arguing for an acceptance of openly practising homosexual ministers. However, such a position does not satisfy those who see it as essentially discriminatory, given that heterosexual ministers have the option of expressing their sexuality through marriage, something not available to the homosexual minister other than through dishonesty, both to self and partner. Is this what the Church wants and expects?

What Now?

In this chapter we have surveyed the Church's debate on this subject over the past fifty years. As with the topic of sex in general there is, nowadays, much more openness and a recognition, even within the Church, that homosexuals are not 'other people out there'. I have a memory of a public scandal many years ago surrounding a minister who was engaging in homosexual activity. The records indicate that he was a commissioner to General Assemblies during the 1950s. Whether he was present at the time of the debates on homosexuality, or even took part in them, I do not know, but what his situation shows clearly is that, in those debates, the Assembly was not talking about other people, but about some of its own.

It is also relevant to reflect on the parallels, though the two situations are very different, with another question which divided the Church in the 1950s, namely, women in the ministry. Those who argued against such a thing also relied on Biblical texts, for example, the instruction that women should be silent in Church, and on the traditions, practice and expectations of many centuries. Then, as noted in Chapter 6, in 1963 the General Assembly was faced with a petition from Miss Mary Lusk, Deaconess (subsequently the Reverend Mary Levison) seeking ordination to the ministry. The petition was remitted to the Panel on Doctrine, and five years later the General Assembly passed the legislation which opened the ministry to women.[25]

Will the Church travel the same journey in relation to people who come forward, eminently suitable for ministry in every way, and who acknowledge that they are homosexual? Or is their case so entirely different that their sexuality cancels out everything else? If so, is the answer to the Moderator's question, 'Yes, they do have some deficiency which is irremediable'? Or, could there come a time when the Church is prepared to countenance an openly gay but celibate person in ministry and be as 'utterly untroubled' as Professor Torrance at such a prospect? Will there even be a time when the Church, having looked again at the Biblical texts and adapted gradually to changing social values, might countenance a committed same-sex couple in the Manse? The Board of Practice and Procedure, in responding to the Government's proposed equality regulations, designed to give effect to the European Directive regarding equality in the employment sphere, sought and obtained an exemption 'in situations where the conduct of someone covered by the regulations would offend the religious susceptibilities of a significant number of the church's followers'. At the same time the Board made clear

> that the Church's position on a wide range of issues, including sexual orientation, is not static, but it should be for churches to debate and resolve these issues in the light of Scripture, tradition and theology, and not under fear that its policies on moral issues will be held to be illegal by the law of the land.[26]

In recent years, seeing how divisive this issue has been for other churches the Church of Scotland has taken a cautious approach, legitimately setting a high value on the Church's unity. Many wonder how long that position can be maintained. Something which could bring matters to a head would be a shifting of the focus from 'issue' to 'person'. Indeed, someone once rebuked me for referring to the 'issue' of homosexuality, on the grounds that we were not talking about an issue but people. I accepted the rebuke. What concentrated Kirk minds on women in the ministry was the appearance of a highly qualified and eminently gifted woman asking to be ordained. Indeed, in her book, *Wrestling with the Church*, Mary Levison quotes from a speech made in support of her petition by the Reverend Campbell Maclean, in which he said: 'The Church has been all too clearly allowed the luxury of indecision and equivocation precisely because it is dealing with a general subject.' The Church was now being challenged by the particularity of the Petition: 'How do we deal with the claim of this particular woman's demands upon the Church?' Mary Levison also notes the opinion of Dr Roy Sanderson, who argued that:

> the Petitioner raised in an acute and responsible way the central issue, which was the possibility of a woman receiving a call and the testing of that call by the Church; that, rather than a theoretical discussion of women's place in the Church, was the question before them.[27]

In a similar way, it is not difficult to imagine a scenario today, where a candidate for ministry, who was quite open about his or her homosexuality, was, on the basis of the approved criteria of assessment applied under the selection procedures, considered acceptable for ministry. The selectors would then have to decide whether to allow the person to proceed in the normal way, or to refer the matter to the Assembly for clarification. A variation on this theme could be a decision by the selectors not to accept the individual, solely on the grounds of sexuality, leading the candidate to petition the Assembly for permission to proceed. Faced with such a petition the Assembly, following the precedent of the Lusk petition, could grant or dismiss the petition, or perhaps set up a Special Commission to report and advise a future General Assembly.

There is no denying the bitterly divisive potential of these matters for the Church. There are Christians who clearly see homosexual behaviour as sinful, and even homosexual orientation as something to be viewed with great suspicion. At the same time others identify the real sin as the discrimination against and demonisation of homosexual persons by society, and by the Church itself. As long ago as 1983 the General Assembly commended a report from the Board of Social Responsibility which stated:

> The Church has a serious responsibility to work towards the elimination of any injustice perpetrated on homosexuals by society. As a group that has suffered more than its share of oppression and contempt, the homosexual community has its particular claim upon the concern of the Church.[28]

The Board's 1994 report (again commended by the Assembly) expressed the view that 'there are grounds for concluding that our culture is homophobic' and went on to observe that 'many "liberals" and "conservatives" are united in calling for respect for members of the homosexual community and in condemning any kind of stigmatisation'.[29] It is much to be desired that the same 'liberals' and 'conservatives' will also make every effort to ensure that disagreements over this sensitive human issue do not destroy the peace of the Church and shatter their unity in Christ.

NOTES

1   Assembly Reports, 1955, p. 375.
2   Assembly Reports, 1956, p. 373.
3   Assembly Reports, 1956, p. 374.
4   Assembly Reports, 1956, p. 375.
5   Assembly Reports, 1958, p. 418.
6   Assembly Reports, 1958, p. 458.
7   See Assembly Reports, 1967, p. 511.
8   Assembly Reports, 1967, p. 512.
9   Assembly Reports, 1967, p. 515.
10 Assembly Reports, 1968, p. 490.
11 Assembly Reports, 1968, p. 490.
12 Assembly Reports, 1983, p. 305.
13 Assembly Reports, 1983, pp. 305–6.
14 Assembly Reports, 1983, p. 308.
15 Assembly Reports, 1994, p. 268.
16 Assembly Reports, 1994, pp. 281–2.
17 Assembly Reports, 1994, p. 257.
18 *The Herald*, 25 May 2000.
19 *The Herald*, 3 July 2003.
20 Supplementary Reports, 2000, p. 36/23.
21 Mark Macaskill, in the *Sunday Times*, © Times Newspapers Syndication, London, 29 June 2003.
22 Mark Macaskill, in the *Sunday Times*, © Times Newspapers Syndication, London, 13 July 2003.
23 The *Scotsman*, 9 July 2003.
24 The *Scotsman*, 15 July 2003.
25 A fuller account of this is given in Chapter 6, on Ministry.
26 Assembly Reports, 2003, p. 1/7.

27 Mary Levison, *Wrestling with the Church*, Arthur James, 1992, pp. 67–8.
28 Assembly Reports, 1983, p. 308.
29 Assembly Reports, 1994, p. 515.

10

Change and the Church's Doctrine

As noted in the Introduction, this chapter is quite 'heavy' in terms of theological and constitutional content. It looks at a complex tangle of issues which lie behind the deceptively simple question: 'What does the Church believe?'

This question came before the General Assembly of 1968 and was to engage the Church in six years of intense debate. However, before going into all of that, some introductory background is called for.

A HISTORICAL SURVEY

The supreme doctrinal standard of the Church of Scotland, as for other reformed Churches, is to be found in the Bible. The great impulse which lay behind the Reformation in the sixteenth century was a fresh reading of Scripture by people such as Martin Luther and John Calvin. Their studies led them to the conclusion that the Church was in need of radical reform and they set about achieving that reformation. In 1560, following the death of the Queen Regent, Mary of Guise, the Scottish Parliament declared Scotland to be a Protestant nation and asked six Protestant ministers, led by John Knox, to draft a Confession of Faith. Within four days they had produced *The Scots Confession*. This set out under twenty-five headings (such as 'God', 'Original Sin', 'The Resurrection' and 'The Right Administration of the Sacraments') the faith and teaching of the Church. In August 1560 the *Confession* was adopted by the Parliament as 'doctrine grounded upon the infallible Word of God'. *The Scots Confession* continues today as a document 'held in honour [by the Church] as having an important place in the history of Scottish Presbyterianism'.[1]

As we have seen, in the decades following the Reformation there was a constant struggle within the reformed Church between Presbyterianism and Episcopalianism, a struggle which was not finally resolved until 1690. As part of this process there was a movement in the 1640s to unite the reformed churches within Great Britain under a Presbyterian form of government. Integral to this enterprise was an Assembly held at Westminster comprising politicians and divines and with five Scottish ministers in attendance. This Westminster Assembly produced a series of impressive documents, namely, the *Form of Presbyterian Church Government*, a *Directory for the Public Worship of God*, *The Confession of Faith*, the *Larger Catechism* and the *Shorter Catechism*. Of these the one that most concerns us here is *The Confession of Faith*, often referred to as 'The Westminster Confession'.

This was a much fuller document than the earlier *Scots Confession* which, as we have seen, was drawn up by six men in the space of four days. The Westminster Assembly had 150 members and its work was carried forward in no fewer than 1,163 sessions spread over six years. *The Book of Confessions* of the Presbyterian Church (USA) comments that:

> The Westminster Standards represent the fruits of a Protestant scholasticism that refined and systematized the teachings of the Reformation. The standards lift up the truth and authority of the Scriptures, as immediately inspired in Hebrew and Greek, kept pure for all ages, and known through the internal witness of the Holy Spirit.[2]

The theology of the Westminster Confession was strong on divine sovereignty and the doctrine of double predestination. This latter taught that from the very beginning some were destined for salvation and others for damnation and that they were powerless to alter in any way this predetermined fate.

The Westminster Confession was adopted by the General Assembly of 1647, the Assembly 'judging it to be most orthodox and grounded upon the Word of God'. It was also ratified by Acts of the Scottish Parliament in 1649 and 1690, becoming, in effect, a foundation document of the Presbyterian Church established by law in the latter year. The 1690 Act described the Confession 'as the public and avowed Confession of this Church, containing the sum and substance of the doctrine of the Reformed Church'.[3] A further Act of 1693 required ministers to declare the Confession to be the confession of their own faith and the doctrine therein contained to be the true doctrine to which they would constantly adhere.

However, within twenty years, largely for reasons reflecting the politics of the day, which were concerned to exclude those with Episcopalian sympathies, a much more rigid formula was prescribed. The General Assembly of 1710 passed an Act for Preserving the Purity of Doctrine and this forbad the venting of opinions

> contrary to any head or article of the said Confession . . . or [the] use [of] any expressions in relation to the Articles of Faith, not agreeable to the form of sound words expressed in the Word of God and the Confession of Faith and Catechisms of this Church, which are the most valuable pieces of her Reformation.

The following year, 1711, the Assembly went further and passed an Act prescribing questions to be put to ministers on ordination and induction. The second question asked:

> Do you sincerely own and believe the whole doctrine of the Confession of Faith . . . to be the truths of God contained in the Scriptures of the Old and New Testaments? And do you own the whole doctrine therein contained as the confession of your faith?

Note the shift from the 1690 statement that the Confession contained the sum and substance of the doctrine of the Reformed Church to the position, twenty years later, whereby individual ministers were required to sign up to it personally, and in its entirety, as the truths of God.

In Chapter 1 we noted that the eighteenth century saw two major secessions in the established church and also further division over the 'new light' controversy. The light in question was to be seen in the tremendous growth of new ideas. After all, this was the age of the Enlightenment, with Edinburgh the Athens of the north and Scotland the intellectual powerhouse of the world. It would have been odd, indeed, had ministers and church members been unaffected by these developments. Given the spirit of the age, many were finding doctrines such as double predestination increasingly difficult to take seriously.

There are even stories told of ministers subscribing to the Confession adding the initials 'E.E.' (errors excepted) after their names.

This was the period of two parties in the Church – Moderates and Evangelicals. The former embraced the new culture and expressed their faith within it; the latter viewed new thinking with suspicion and stood by what they understood to be the timeless truths of the gospel expressed in the Confession. The new light mindset is perfectly illustrated in the 1804 'revised testimony' of the new light anti-burghers (one of the secession church groupings). This stated in connection with the Confession:

> That, as no human composure, however, excellent and well expressed, can be supposed to contain a full and comprehensive view of divine truth; so by this adherence [to the Confession of Faith] we are not precluded from embracing, upon due deliberation, any further light which may afterward arise from the Word of God about any article of divine truth.[4]

Again, as we have noted, the nineteenth century brought both division and reunion to the Church. In 1843 the Disruption resulted in the departure of around one-third of the ministers and congregations of the Established Church to form the Free Church. Four years later, a number of the eighteenth-century secession churches came together to form the United Presbyterian Church. In all three Presbyterian churches controversy over the relationship of the Church to the Westminster Confession rumbled on. In 1860 the Moderator of the Established Church Assembly reminded commissioners that 'our Confession . . . was accepted as the truth of God and the Church was . . . not free at any time to modify, alter, or depart from it, nor to hold the truth of any of its doctrines in question'. This hard-line declaration provoked Professor Tulloch of St Andrews University and seventy other commissioners to protest that 'the old relation of our Church to the Confession cannot continue'.[5]

However, it was within the United Presbyterian Church that the first serious steps towards reform were taken. Three main factors were influencing reflective minds at the time. There was the rise of Biblical criticism and a questioning of the literal nature of Scriptural truth. Second, increased missionary work overseas (this was the age of David Livingstone and Mary Slessor) rendered increasingly unsustainable the notion that those who had never heard the Gospel were doomed to eternal damnation. The third factor had to do with Church–State relations. The Confession was not only part of the law of the Church, but also part of the law of the land, given that the Church of Scotland was established by law. Many, especially within the Free and United Presbyterian Churches, found this unsatisfactory and felt that the Church should not be so tied to the State.

A United Presbyterian minister, Fergus Ferguson, was prominent among those calling for a fresh look at the relationship between the Church and the Confession. Ferguson clearly had his supporters. After achieving some notoriety, and being subject to a presbytery investigation during his ministry in Dalkeith, he was called to a new church at Queen's Park in Glasgow. There he again came under investigation and when, eventually, he was called before the Presbytery on a charge of heresy, his congregation increased his stipend and prepared to secede in the event of his deposition! Ferguson was not a man to mince his words. He once characterised the Confession as 'no exhibition of the Divine order of the universe, but an exhibition, at least in part, of the disorder of the human intellect'.[6] What he sought was liberty to investigate, fully and freely, everything in God's revelation, whether consistent or not with the so-called standards of the faith.

As a result of the questions raised by men like Ferguson the United Presbyterian Church, in 1879, adopted a Declaratory Act setting out its understanding of the Confession and the relationship to it of the Church and its ministers. This Act acknowledged that the Confession was of 'human composition' and, so, 'necessarily imperfect'. It declared 'that the doctrine of divine decrees [predestination] … is held in connection and harmony with the truth that God is not willing that any should perish …'. The Act also, while emphasising salvation in Christ, declared that

> in accepting the Standards, it is not required to be held that any who die in infancy are lost, or that God may not extend His grace to any who are without the pale of ordinary means, as it may seem good in his sight.

In such ways the Act clearly addressed the concerns of those troubled by the doctrine of double predestination. It also recognised liberty of opinion on matters 'not entering into the substance of the faith', finding an illustration of this in the 'interpretation of the "six days" in the Mosaic account of the creation'.

Meanwhile within the Free Church similar moves were afoot. The main focus there was an Old Testament scholar and professor, Robertson Smith. In 1870, at the young age of twenty-four, Robertson Smith was appointed to the chair of Old Testament at Aberdeen. Warning signs were apparent in his inaugural lecture, in which he likened the Bible to 'the garment of Christ' and went on to point out that 'we do not lay hold of Christ by grasping his garment'. The key to proper study and interpretation of the Scriptures was, in his view, 'that we are to seek in the Bible, not a body of abstract religious truths, but the personal history of God's gracious dealings with men'.[7] This somewhat conflicted with the Confession's view of the Scriptures as 'infallible truth'.

Five years later Smith had an article on the Bible published in the *Encyclopaedia Britannica.* Among other things this questioned the Mosaic authorship of the Pentateuch (the first five books of the Old Testament) and rejected the superhuman reality of angels as a popular assumption, rather than a doctrine of revelation. The Free Church College Committee investigated and, while concluding that there was not enough in the article to warrant a heresy trial, nevertheless considered it to be 'of a dangerous and unsettling tendency'.[8] Questions were also raised as to Smith's continuing suitability as a teacher of divinity students. The controversy rumbled on and eventually in 1881 the Free Church Assembly removed Smith from his chair. Within a short time, this brilliant man was appointed joint-editor of the *Encyclopaedia Britannica* and two years later he became Professor of Arabic at Cambridge – a real loss to Scotland.

What all of this showed was that the Westminster Confession was inadequate to the needs of the day. In an earlier age it would have been possible to judge an allegation of heresy by reference to the Confession, but now it was the Confession itself which was being challenged. Indeed, scholars like Robertson Smith were even raising questions about the nature and authorship of Scripture itself. The issue attracted huge public interest, with crowds queuing to get into the Assembly Hall to follow the debate and witness the human dramas unfolding. It is recorded that people queued from six in the morning to hear Robertson Smith defend himself before the General Assembly (and to be instructed by him!). There was also much media interest. In a leading article of the period, the *Scotsman* argued 'that it is one of the advantages of a Free Church that it has absolute power over its own creed'; and that 'while the Established Church must confess they are bound by the fetters of the law, the Free Church is not so bound'.[9]

Faced with these pressures the Free Church decided to follow the line taken by the United Presbyterian Church and prepare a Declaratory Act, setting out its own understanding of and relationship to the Confession. This was finally approved by the General Assembly of 1892 and was similar in approach and content to the United Presbyterian Act of thirteen years earlier. However, this move did not meet with universal acceptance within the Free Church. In fact it led to yet another secession when, the following year, the Free Presbyterian Church came into being, taking its stand on adherence 'to the Bible in its entirety as the Word of God and to the Confession of Faith in all its doctrines as hitherto held by the Free Church'. To prevent an even greater secession the Free Church passed a further Declaratory Act in 1894 which made it clear that the 1892 Act was not intended to impose new doctrinal statements upon any who were content to uphold the traditional view of the Confession. After all, liberty of opinion worked both ways. Nevertheless the facility for subscribing to the Confession 'in view of' the Declaratory Acts afforded relief to many and enabled the Free Church, in the words of Professor Burleigh, 'to make an outstanding contribution to theological scholarship and to Scotland's reputation for Christian learning'.[10]

The *Scotsman* leader, quoted above, pointed out that the freedom enjoyed by the Free Church (and also by the United Presbyterian Church) was not available to the Established Church. Legal opinion had acknowledged that the Church was free

like other corporations, to make bye-laws – not to alter or repeal, but to enforce and promote the objects of their institution, in so far only, however, as these may be consistent with the provisions of the statutes under which they are constituted.[11]

Erskine, in his *Institutes of the Law of Scotland*, put it even more bluntly when he insisted that resolutions of the Church concerning matters of faith and doctrine 'be consistent with the laws of the realm from which our National Church derives its whole authority'.[12] Such a view was anathema to many. Did the Church not derive its authority from Christ, its sole King and Head? Yet, the clear inference from such legal opinion was that the Established Church was not free to follow the example of its sister churches and adjust its relationship to the Westminster Confession.

Be that as it may, the debate certainly took place within the Established Church as in the other two Presbyterian denominations. One of the principal causes of agitation was the requirement that elders indicate their acceptance of a document which they had never read. (How many elders today have read the Westminster Confession?) A committee was set up to look into the matter and reported to the General Assembly in 1888. It offered a different approach from the Declaratory Acts favoured by the other churches. Rather, it focused on the formula of subscription which had been in place since 1711 and recommended that the Church revert to the earlier and less rigid formula of 1693. This earlier formula had sought an acknowledgement that the doctrine *contained in* the Confession was the true doctrine, whereas the 1711 formula had required assent to 'the whole doctrine of the Confession' as 'the truths of God contained in the Scriptures of the Old and New Testaments'. That opinion was divided on the matter is apparent from the fact that this proposal was carried by only five votes and the matter was sent to presbyteries for their consideration under the Barrier Act.[13] A majority of presbyteries approved and the ensuing General Assembly then passed the necessary legislation.

Through all of this controversy the division of Presbyterian Scotland into three churches was increasingly perceived as unsatisfactory. In the second half of the nineteenth century the prospect of union between the Free and United Presbyterian Churches was explored and in 1900 this came about with the formation of the United Free Church. A small group within the Free Church opposed the union (the 'Wee Frees', as they came to be known) and carried its opposition to the point of taking legal action to establish their claim that they, and not the majority who supported union, were the true heirs of the Disruption tradition and therefore entitled to all the assets of their Church. The case took four years until, in 1904, the House of Lords ruled in their favour. This created a chaotic situation. The tiny dissenting minority could not possibly use all the buildings that were legally declared to be theirs and the majority was not exactly pleased to be deprived of what they regarded as their property. The knife was further twisted in the wound when the minority offered the use of college properties to the united church on condition that the teaching given in them was strictly in accordance with the Confession! The anger and frustration of the new United Free Church is summed up by one of its leaders and an architect of the union, Principal Robert Rainy:

> The idea with which some of these distinguished men seem to be content, the idea of a Church consenting to be held absolutely and for ever by the faith of men who died two hundred and fifty years ago – good men, no doubt, – that idea is simply to be denounced as ungodly.[14]

As far as Rainy was concerned 'the only authentic Free Church tradition is the right of the Church to determine its own constitution, its own principles, its own doctrine'.[15]

Eventually the only way to resolve the crisis was for a Parliamentary Commission to be given the task of achieving an equitable distribution of the pre-1900 Free Church properties and this process was provided for by the Churches (Scotland) Act of 1905. Eventually matters were settled but the opportunity was also taken by the new United Free Church to declare the spiritual independence of the Church. This was done by an Act of its General Assembly of 1906, known as The United Free Church Act anent the Spiritual Independence of the Church. This asserts the Church's freedom 'to alter, change, add to or modify her constitution and laws, subordinate standards and formulas and to determine and declare what these are',[16] and remains part of the constitution of the Church of Scotland today.

As well as providing for an equitable distribution of properties, the 1905 Churches (Scotland) Act also dealt with the issue of spiritual independence. There was incorporated in the Act a clause which provided that the formula of subscription to the Westminster Confession in the Established Church should be a matter for that Church's General Assembly. It is, again, a measure of the public interest in the matter that in 1907 the *Glasgow Herald* published a series of articles from 'leading Scottish ministers' on the general subject of 'Creed Revision in Scotland – its Necessity and Scope'. Some argued for a revision of the Westminster Confession; others favoured an attempt to prepare a new confession of faith altogether; others again sought refuge in the ancient creeds of the Church. Eventually, in 1910, the Church of Scotland approved a new formula for both ministers and elders in which they declared: 'I hereby subscribe the Confession of Faith, declaring that I accept it as the Confession of this Church and that I believe the fundamental doctrines of the Christian Faith contained therein.' We have come a long way from 1711 when the Confession in its entirety was subscribed as a statement of personal belief.

By this time there was a strong climate of opinion that the 1900 union of the Free and United Presbyterian Churches should be followed by another union involving the established church. In October 1910 a programme for negotiations was agreed and it was recognised that the two great questions were spiritual independence and the national recognition of religion. A detailed and masterly account of the negotiations is given by the late Dr Douglas Murray in his *Rebuilding the Kirk: Presbyterian Re-union in Scotland, 1909–1929*.[17] Suffice it to say here that a key outcome of the process was agreement (after much debate) on 'Articles Declaratory of the Constitution of the Church of Scotland in Matters Spiritual' (the Declaratory Articles). These were adopted by the General Assemblies of both Churches and thereafter incorporated as a Schedule to an Act of Parliament, the Church of Scotland Act of 1921. The Articles asserted the spiritual independence of the Church from the state and thus offered a very different model of 'establishment' from the Church of England. The Church was recognised as 'a national church' with a 'distinctive call and duty to bring the ordinances of religion to the people in every parish of Scotland through a territorial ministry' (Article III). The first article offered a statement of belief, but did not claim this to be exhaustive, preferring to affirm simply that the Church 'receives the Word of God which is contained in the Scriptures of the Old and New Testaments as its supreme rule of faith and life; and avows the fundamental doctrines of the Catholic faith founded thereupon' (Article I). The Westminster Confession was highlighted as the Church's 'principal subordinate standard' (Article II) and described as 'containing the sum and substance of the Faith of the Reformed Church'. The freedom to adjust the Church's relationship to its doctrinal standards, set out in the United Free Church Act of 1906, was reaffirmed as was 'liberty of opinion in points which do not enter into the substance of the faith' (Article V). This principle had been enshrined in the Declaratory Acts of 1879 and 1892, though the later Free Church Act had preferred the expression 'diversity of opinion'. With regard to the questions put to ministers on ordination and induction and the signing of the formula, the phrase used in connection with the Confession sought an assurance that the candidate believed 'the fundamental doctrines of the Christian faith contained in the Confession of Faith of this Church'.

So it came about that on 2 October 1929 the United Free Church and the Church of Scotland united under the name 'The Church of Scotland'. On the basis of reservations over any state connection, a minority from within the United Free Church felt unable to accede to the union and so that denomination continues to the present. Similarly the Free and Free Presbyterian Churches continue with new seceding groups emerging from both in recent years. However, in this great 1929 reunion was gathered up and reconciled much of the division which for nigh on two centuries had so scarred the face of the Kirk by Law Established.

THE CONFESSIONAL CONTROVERSY 1968–1974 AND ITS AFTERMATH

And so to the General Assembly of 1968, and the question with which we began this chapter. What does the Church believe? The question came before that Assembly in two different ways and the asking of it was to lead to a six-year debate which raised again many of the issues which we have just explored.

Professor J. K. S. Reid of the Chair of Systematic Theology at Aberdeen University successfully moved that the Panel on Doctrine be instructed

> to give consideration to the place of the Westminster Confession of Faith as the subordinate standard of the Church's faith and to the reference to it in the preamble and questions used at ordination, with a view to offering guidance to the Church.

In speaking to this Professor Reid referred to a comment by the Lord High Commissioner (Lord Reith) in his opening address to the Assembly. Lord Reith had made reference to the uncertainties of the age. The 'uncertainties' in question, he indicated, arose from the debates generated at the time by books such as the Bishop of Woolwich's *Honest to God* which many found challenging to their faith. If bishops were speculating over the nature of such matters as the virgin birth, the miracles and the resurrection, what were ordinary church members to believe?

'Believe your faith', Lord Reith had urged. 'Let the Church affirm the eternal verities.' 'But what faith and which verities?' Professor Reid wondered. He recalled a case where a member of the Presbytery of Aberdeen had been accused of uttering doctrinal statements 'felt to be at variance with the standards of the Church', and yet it had proved extremely difficult to pinpoint what these standards were and therefore in what ways the minister's statements deviated from them.

Professor Reid was seconded by Dr Nevile Davidson, minister of Glasgow Cathedral. Dr Davidson identified the problem this way:

> A confession of faith, which does not completely reflect the theological thinking and Christian conviction of the Church which professes it cannot be of the full use to the Church which it ought to be, and I think that is the position with the Westminster Confession at the moment.[18]

Dr Davidson went on to list three purposes of a confession of faith: (1) to safeguard sound doctrine; (2) for the instruction of enquirers and new members; and (3) to serve as a declaration of what the Church believes. On all three counts he held that the Westminster Confession failed to meet the needs of the present day.

At the same time there was presented an Overture from the Presbytery of Glasgow. The aim of this was to make the Church's doctrinal statements more widely known and the impetus behind it, the Assembly was told, had come from a petition to the Presbytery from members of a Kirk Session expressing concern at the 'confusion and distress in the minds of many Church members arising from uncertainty about what the Church's "official belief" is'. Speaking to the petition the Reverend H. C. Thomson pointed out that the Church's doctrine was set forth in the Confession and the Declaratory Articles, but these documents were not generally available. While there was, he acknowledged, an admirable summary in the preamble to the ordination service, opportunities for church members to hear this were inevitably somewhat limited. There was thus a lack of clarity as to what the faith of the Church was. Dr Andrew Herron, Clerk to Glasgow Presbytery, spoke in support of Dr Thomson. He pointed out that extravagant statements attracted publicity ('minister denies resurrection!') and there was a feeling that the Church was unable to deal with heresy because it was unable to define orthodoxy. The Overture asked that the Assembly 'appoint a Committee to consider and report upon what steps should be taken to bring to the notice of ministers and members of the Church that the Church's "official belief" is set forth in Article I of the Articles Declaratory and in the Preamble, and to impress upon all concerned the necessity of adhering to these basic affirmations of the Church's faith'. It is interesting to note that, whereas the nineteenth-century controversies were led largely by a demand for greater freedom in understanding and expressing the faith, the concern now being expressed was that this freedom had gone too far.

The General Assembly accepted both Professor Reid's proposal and the Glasgow Overture. The following year the Panel on Doctrine reported back and acknowledged that the situation was unsatisfactory. From being bound strictly to a Confession the Church was now committed only to a largely undefined 'sum and substance of the faith', combined with a considerable degree of liberty of opinion. The report indicated that the Panel had considered drafting a new Confession of Faith altogether, but had felt unable to undertake such a task without a specific instruction to do so. The Panel also remarked that it was doubtful whether such an attempt would be wise 'in this period of ecumenical change and theological ferment'.[19] What it proposed was, arguably, more radical, namely, that the Church should consider abandoning altogether the concept of a subordinate standard, that the preamble read at ordination services should be amended to include a brief statement of fundamental doctrines and that all references to liberty of opinion should be dropped. The formula would be revised to open with the words, 'I believe the fundamental doctrines of the Christian Faith affirmed in this Preamble . . .' The proposed new Preamble would include the statement: 'The Church of Scotland acknowledges and is guided by the Apostles' Creed and the Nicene Creed, and by the Scots Confession and the Westminster Confession of Faith as historic statements of the Church's abiding faith.'

These proposals were sent to presbyteries for discussion and comment. The responses indicated that a small majority of presbyteries (thirty out of fifty-four) favoured the concept of departing from the idea of a subordinate standard, while only eighteen out of fifty-four wished to have a new or revised Confession of Faith. Thirty-six out of fifty-four were content with the proposed statement of fundamental beliefs. However, the issue was not simply doctrinal since a legal challenge had been raised as to the competence of the Church thus altering its relationship to the Westminster Confession. The Procurator's Opinion was that it was perfectly competent for the Church, in terms of its spiritual independence, so to proceed. The Panel argued, further, that not to proceed would risk regarding the Confession not as a subordinate standard but as, effectively, the supreme standard. It was, it maintained, important to distinguish between 'the substance of the faith' and expressions of the faith in propositional forms.

> All our formulations [the 1970 report argued] are made in the light of Scripture, but in such a way that they point beyond themselves to Jesus Christ. There is always the danger that we present our formulations of the Truth as the Truth. We think it important therefore to distinguish between Confessions of the Faith and

Definitions of the Faith; the latter we believe to be beyond human power adequately to frame.[20]

While the wider Church seemed encouraging of the new Preamble and statement of fundamental beliefs, there was real alarm over the prospect of departing from the principle of liberty of opinion. Indeed, was this not to do the very thing the Panel cautioned against and seek to frame an unassailable verbal definition of the faith, which even to question would attract a charge of heresy? Eventually, the proposal to remove liberty of opinion was withdrawn and further work was undertaken on the revised preamble. By 1971 the number of presbyteries in favour of abandoning the idea of a subordinate standard had increased to forty-six, with twelve against. Kirk Sessions were also asked the same question and responded by a margin of 1,146 to 259 in favour. The statement of fundamental doctrines also scored high approval ratings. Eventually the whole matter was referred to presbyteries under the procedure for amending the Declaratory Articles. This requires reference to presbyteries in two successive years with a two-thirds majority in favour in both years. This considerable hurdle was successfully cleared with a majority in favour, the first time of forty-three to eighteen and in the second year of forty-nine to twelve. With this favourable wind behind them, the new Preamble, Questions and Formula came for final consideration by the General Assembly of 1974. However, there was again strong opposition, much of it on legal grounds led by Professor Francis Lyall of the Faculty of Law at Aberdeen University. The National Church Association had acquired a contrary legal opinion to that given to the Panel by the Procurator. The spectre of the Free Church case was raised with the prospect of a disaffected minority regarding itself as the faithful remnant and successfully pursuing a legal title to the name and entire assets of the Church of Scotland. The new Procurator, C. K. Davidson, shared the view of his predecessor, W. R. Grieve, that this was unlikely, though not impossible. He was quite convinced that the arrangements for safeguarding the Church's spiritual independence, which underpinned the 1929 union, intended that the Church should have the widest scope for further amendment of its constitutional documents. In the event, the Panel's proposals faced a counter-motion proposed and seconded by former moderator Dr Andrew Herron and future moderator Dr Duncan Shaw, as formidable a combination of constitutionalist and church historian as could be imagined. They moved that the Church should depart from the matter until such a time as a new statement of faith was produced and, notwithstanding the considerable support for the new proposals across the Church, they carried the day by a majority of 292 votes to 238.

As well as working on the status of the Westminster Confession the Panel had also been giving attention to the matter of a statement of faith for popular use. This, it will be recalled, was the burden of the Overture from Glasgow back in 1968. Faced with the collapse of all its work on the Confession, the Panel, stoically, proposed to continue with this project, an intention confirmed by the General Assembly. A draft was presented to the Assembly of 1976 and was then sent to presbyteries for consideration. However, it did not find favour, tending to fall between two stools. Some wanted a short, dogmatic test of orthodoxy, while others wished to see what nowadays we would call a 'user-friendly' pastoral and teaching tool. Sensing a seemingly impossible task the Panel came back to the Assembly in 1978 and asked to be relieved from this remit. It pointed the Church to the first of the Declaratory Articles 'as an authoritative guide in any statement of Christian belief' and asked merely that it be left with a general remit 'to report to a future General Assembly with, if so advised, new proposals anent the definition of the Church's doctrinal standards'.

While content to release the Panel from the remit to produce a popular statement of belief and to refer the Church to the first Declaratory Article the Assembly insisted on instructing the Panel anew 'to consider the status of the Westminster Confession as the Church's subordinate standard'. An attempt to revise the Formula of Subscription was received by the General Assembly of 1984, but failed to secure the support of a majority of presbyteries under the Barrier Act. In 1986 the Panel was instructed to prepare a new Statement of Faith and this resulted in the General Assembly of 1992 authorising a contemporary Statement of Faith for use in worship and teaching. This is printed inside the back cover of *Common Order*, 1994, and also as an appendix to this chapter. Much work had gone into the preparation of this Statement, again involving intensive discussions across the Church. In presenting a final draft for authorisation the Panel on Doctrine declared its aim to have been 'to provide a Statement which will make the basis of faith intelligible to outsiders and which the large majority within the Kirk is able to affirm without too much decoding and interpretation'. At the same time the Panel emphasised that there was no intention that the Statement 'should in any way replace the ancient Creeds or the Westminster Confession, or that it should establish a new test of orthodoxy'. Consideration, the Assembly was told, was still being given to address the concern for a modern confession of faith.[21]

There is little doubt that the General Assembly of 1974 missed a great opportunity to modernise the Church's doctrinal position. The Westminster Confession has great theological and historical significance, as do the Scots Confession and the ancient creeds, yet it is raised above these as the Church's 'principal subordinate standard'. At the same time, the Church's relationship to this standard is hedged about by the nineteenth-century Declaratory Acts, by an Assembly Act of 1986 dissociating the Church from the Confession's seventeenth-century anti-Catholic rhetoric, and by liberty of opinion on points which do not enter into the substance of the faith. This is hardly a satisfactory position for a principal subordinate standard and, in my view, it would have been better had the Confession been accorded its place of honour with the other historic creeds.[22] This is not to say that present arrangements are entirely unsatisfactory. The first Declaratory Article, the historic statements and liberty of opinion together offer the basis for a broad church and it is simply not the case that we do not know what we believe. At the end of the day faith is expressed in the real lives of Christian disciples, affirming that Jesus Christ is Lord and seeking to follow him. Credal and confessional statements are enormously helpful, but given the pace of change in our world and the continuing discovery of more of the secrets of the universe, it is important that the Church be able to articulate its faith afresh and anew as new questions arise. The time is coming when the Church should take up the unfinished business of 1974.

Finally, we must note the supreme standard of faith and life 'contained in the Scriptures of the Old and New Testaments'. The phrase 'contained in' is crucial here as it is in relation to the 'sum and substance of the faith contained in' the Confession. The Church does not hold that the words of the Bible constitute the infallible Word of God, though, being a broad church, any member of the Church is free to believe that. What they are not free to do is insist that everyone else believes the same! The Church interprets Scripture under the guidance of the Holy Spirit and has concluded, for example, notwithstanding certain things which are written in the Bible, that ministers should, subject to certain conditions, be allowed to re-marry divorced persons in Church and that women may be ordained to ministry and eldership. As previously noted, the Church has also interpreted the Confession and decided that various statements within it are not part of the 'sum and substance' of the faith. This demonstrates that the Church is a living community, seeking faithfully and prayerfully to understand God's Word in the present moment and to be guided by it.

What then does the Church believe? The key summary continues to be found in the first of the Declaratory Articles, with the Westminster Confession (subject to the various historical qualifications noted in this chapter), as repository of the 'fundamental doctrines of the Christian faith'. Over and above these the Word of God, 'contained in the Scriptures of the Old and New Testaments' remains 'the supreme rule of faith and life'.

APPENDIX 1: ARTICLE 1 OF THE ARTICLES DECLARATORY OF THE CONSTITUTION OF THE CHURCH OF SCOTLAND IN MATTERS SPIRITUAL

The Church of Scotland is part of the Holy Catholic or Universal Church; worshipping one God, Almighty, all-wise, and all loving, in the Trinity of the Father, the Son, and the Holy Ghost, the same in substance, equal in power and glory; adoring the Father, infinite in Majesty, of whom are all things; confessing our Lord Jesus Christ, the Eternal Son, made very man for our salvation; glorying in His Cross and Resurrection, and owning obedience to Him as Head over all things to His Church; trusting in the promised renewal and guidance of the Holy Spirit; proclaiming the forgiveness of sins and acceptance with God through faith in Christ, and the gift of Eternal Life; and labouring for the advancement of the Kingdom of God throughout the world. The Church of Scotland adheres to the Scottish Reformation: receives the Word of God which is contained in the Scriptures of the Old and New Testaments as its supreme rule of faith and life; and avows the fundamental doctrines of the Catholic faith founded thereupon.

Note: This is the first of nine Articles and such is its importance that the procedures for amending the Articles, set out in the eighth Article, require that any alteration be undertaken 'consistently with the provisions of the first Article hereof, adherence to which, as interpreted by the Church, is essential to its continuity and corporate life'.

All nine Articles are set out in James L. Weatherhead, *The Constitution and Laws of the Church of Scotland*, Edinburgh: Board of Practice and Procedure, Church of Scotland, 1997, pp. 159–61, and can also be found in J. T. Cox, *Practice and Procedure in the Church of Scotland*, 6th edn, ed. D. F. M. MacDonald, Edinburgh: Church of Scotland, 1976, pp. 390–2.

APPENDIX 2: PREAMBLE QUESTIONS AND FORMULA USED IN ORDINATION AND INDUCTION SERVICES

Preamble

In the name of the Lord Jesus Christ, the King and Head of the Church, Who, being ascended on high, has given gifts to God's people for the edifying of the body of Christ, we are met here as a Presbytery to ordain A. B. to the office of the Holy Ministry by prayer and the laying on of hands to the Presbyters to whom it belongs [and to induct him/her to the pastoral charge of . . .].

In this act of ordination the Church of Scotland, as part of the Holy Catholic or Universal Church, worshipping one God – Father, Son and Holy Spirit – affirms anew its belief in the Gospel of the sovereign grace and love of God, wherein through Jesus Christ, His only Son, our Lord, Incarnate, Crucified and Risen, He freely offers to all people, upon repentance and faith, the forgiveness of sins, renewal by the Holy Spirit, and eternal life, and calls them to labour in the fellowship of faith for the advancement of the Kingdom of God throughout the world.

The Church of Scotland acknowledges the Word of God which is contained in the Scriptures of the Old and New Testaments to be the supreme rule of faith and life.

The Church of Scotland holds as its subordinate standard the Westminster Confession of Faith, recognizing liberty of opinion on such points of doctrine as do not enter into the substance of the Faith, and claiming the right, in dependence on the promised guidance of the Holy Spirit, to formulate, interpret, or modify its subordinate standards: always in agreement with the Word of God and the fundamental doctrines of the Christian Faith contained in the said Confession – of which agreement the Church itself shall be sole judge.

Questions to Minister about to be ordained and/or inducted

1. Do you believe in one God – Father, Son and Holy Spirit; and do you confess anew the Lord Jesus Christ as your Saviour and Lord?

2. Do you believe the Word of God, which is contained in the Scriptures of the Old and New Testaments to be the supreme rule of faith and life?

3. Do you believe the fundamental doctrines of the Christian faith contained in the Confession of Faith of this Church?

4. Do you acknowledge the Presbyterian Government of this Church to be agreeable to the Word of God; and do you promise to be subject in the Lord to this Presbytery and to the General Assembly?

5. Do you promise to seek the unity and peace of this Church; to uphold the doctrine, worship, government and discipline thereof; and to cherish a spirit of love towards all your brothers and sisters in Christ?

6. Are not zeal for the glory of God, love to the Lord Jesus Christ, and a desire for the salvation of all people, so far as you know your own heart, your great motives and chief inducements to enter into the office of the Holy Ministry?

7. Do you engage, in the strength of the Lord Jesus Christ, to live a godly and circumspect life; and faithfully, diligently and cheerfully to discharge the duties of your ministry, seeking in all things the advancement of the Kingdom of God?

8. (*To be used at an Induction*) Do you accept and close with the call to be Pastor of this charge and promise, through grace, to study to approve yourself a faithful Minister of the Gospel among this people?

Question to the Congregation at an Induction

Do you, as members and adherents of this Congregation, in receiving A. B., whom you have called to be your Minister promise her/him all due honour and support in the Lord; and, in view of the pastoral and missionary obligations of this congregation, do you each now agree to share with your Minister the responsibility of Christian witness and service; and will you give of your means, as the Lord shall prosper you, for the maintenance of the Christian Ministry and the furtherance of the Gospel?

The Formula which is signed by Ministers, Elders, Deacons and Readers

I believe the fundamental doctrines of the Christian Faith contained in the Confession of Faith of this Church.

I acknowledge the Presbyterian Government of this Church to be agreeable to the Word of God, and promise that I will submit thereto and concur therewith.

I promise to observe the order of worship and the administration of all public ordinances, as the same are or may be allowed in this Church.

APPENDIX 3: A STATEMENT OF CHRISTIAN FAITH, AUTHORISED FOR USE IN WORSHIP AND TEACHING, BY THE GENERAL ASSEMBLY OF 1992

We believe in one God:
    Father, Son and Holy Spirit.
    God is love.

We praise God the Father:
    Who created the universe and keeps it in being.
    He has made us his sons and daughters to share his joy,
    living together in justice and peace,
    caring for his world and for each other.

We proclaim Jesus Christ, God the Son:
    born of Mary,
    by the power of the Holy Spirit,
    he became one of us,
    sharing our life and death.
    He made known God's compassion and mercy,
    giving hope and declaring forgiveness of sin,
    offering healing and wholeness to all.
    By his death on the cross and by his resurrection,
    he has triumphed over evil.
    Jesus is Lord of life and of all creation.

We trust God the Holy Spirit:
    who unites us to Christ
    and gives life to the Church;
    who brings us to repentance
    and assures us of forgiveness.
    The Spirit guides us

in our understanding of the Bible,
renews us in the sacraments,
and calls us to serve God in the world.

We rejoice in the gift of eternal life:
we have sure and certain hope of
resurrection through Christ,
and we look for his coming again
to judge the world.
Then all things will be made new:
and creation will rejoice
in worshipping the Father,
through the Son,
in the power of the Spirit,
one God, blessed for ever.   Amen

NOTES

1 J. T. Cox, *Practice and Procedure in the Church of Scotland*, 6th edn, ed. D. F. M. MacDonald, Edinburgh: Church of Scotland, 1976, p. 389.
2 *The Book of Confessions*, Presbyterian Church (USA), 1999. Used with permission from Westminster John Knox Press.
3 Act Ratifying the Confession of Faith and Settling the Presbyterian Church Government, 1690.
4 Revised Testimony of the New Light Anti-burgher Seceders, 1804.
5 Quoted in A. C. Cheyne, 'The Confession through Three Centuries', in Alasdair I. C. Heron (ed.), *The Westminster Confession in the Church Today*, Edinburgh: Saint Andrew Press, 1982, pp. 17–27 at p. 23.
6 Quoted in J. H. Leckie, *Fergus Ferguson, D.D., His Theology and Heresy Trial*, Edinburgh: T&T Clark, 1923, p. 109.
7 Quoted in Andrew L. Drummond and James Bulloch, *The Church in Late Victorian Scotland, 1874–1900*, Edinburgh: Saint Andrew Press, 1975, p. 48.
8 See P. Carnegie Simpson, *Life of Principal Rainy*, 2 vols, London: Hodder & Stoughton, 1909, Book 1, p. 316.
9 The *Scotsman*, 2 June 1888.
10 J. H. S. Burleigh, *A Church History of Scotland*, London: Oxford University Press, p. 361.
11 Judgement of Lord Cunninghame in the Strathbogie Case, 1843, quoted in Taylor Innes, *The Law of Creeds in Scotland*, Edinburgh and London: Blackwood, 1902, p. 84.

12 Erskine, *Institutes of the Law of Scotland,* 1.5.24.

13 The Barrier Act, passed by the General Assembly of 1697, requires all proposals for innovative legislation in the areas of worship, government, doctrine and discipline, to have the approval of two successive General Assemblies, the approval of a majority of presbyteries being indicated during the intervening year.

14 See Simpson, *Principal Rainy,* p. 366.

15 See G. D. Henderson, *The Claims of the Church of Scotland,* London: Hodder & Stoughton, 1951, p. 115.

16 The Act is set out in Cox, *Practice and Procedure in the Church of Scotland,* 6th edn, pp. 392–433.

17 Douglas M. Murray, *Rebuilding the Kirk: Presbyterian Re-union in Scotland, 1909–1929,* Edinburgh: Scottish Academic Press, 2000.

18 Verbatim Record, General Assembly, 1968, p. 1576.

19 Assembly Reports, 1969, p. 210.

20 Assembly Reports, 1979, pp. 174–5.

21 Assembly Reports, 1992, p. 189.

22 I am grateful to my colleague, the Reverend Douglas Galbraith, Secretary of the Panels of Doctrine and Worship, for drawing my attention to the Basis of Union of the Uniting Church of Australia, which declares as follows: 'The Uniting Church continues to learn of the teaching of the Holy Scriptures in the obedience and freedom of faith, and in the power of the promised gift of the Holy Spirit, from the witness of Reformation Fathers as expressed in various ways in the Scots Confession of Faith (1560), the Heidelberg Catechism (1563), the Westminster Confession of Faith (1647), and the Savoy Declaration (1658). In like manner she will listen to the preaching of John Wesley in his Forty-Four Sermons (1793). She will commit her ministers and instructors to study these statements, so that the congregation of Christ's people may again be reminded of the grace which justifies them through faith, of the centrality of the person and work of Christ the Justifier and of the need for a constant appeal to Holy Scripture' (Paragraph 10).

11

The Kirk in the Twenty-First Century

The general theme of this book has to do with change and the Church. The Church of Scotland entered the twenty-first century in a culture and climate of change. The very arrival of the new millennium was sufficient cause for reflecting on the future and the Overture to the General Assembly of 1999 from the Presbytery of Edinburgh, which was ultimately to lead to the *Church without Walls* report, sought nothing less than a charting of the way into the new millennium. Yet, as we have seen in the previous ten chapters, change has been part of the very essence of the Church, not only over the past half-century surveyed in this book but all down the centuries since the very beginning. Strategic initiatives such as *Church without Walls*, the Committee of Forty and the Anderson Commission have addressed issues of the day, but ultimately they are all expressions of that renewing energy which flows from the Holy Spirit and which is the very light and life of the Church. We can only speculate as to what changes lie ahead for the Church of Scotland over the next half century. I hesitate to offer predictions, but, in this concluding, gathering-up chapter, I offer some thoughts as to the way ahead. Inevitably, these arise from and develop further things discussed in the foregoing chapters.

THE CHURCH'S PERSPECTIVE AND SELF-UNDERSTANDING

I consider it important that the Church of Scotland should maintain a proper historical perspective, thereby continuing to draw nourishment from those deep roots which reach into the Church of Ninian and

Columba. I find it interesting that, while the latter part of the twentieth century has witnessed a diminishing appetite for institutional religion, it has also seen an increasing interest in spirituality. It does not follow that because people turn their backs upon the Church that they have rejected Christian teaching and spiritual values. In particular, devotional material drawn from the Celtic Church has become immensely popular. Gaelic blessings such as 'Deep peace of the running wave to you', the prayer collections of David Adam of Holy Island, the anthologies of Shirley Toulson, the worship resources of the Iona Community's Wild Goose Group all tap into this rich seam and clearly meet both a demand and a need. In our self-understanding as a Church, therefore, we need to be quite clear that we are the Church not only of Chalmers and Knox but also of Ninian and Columba. In the chapter on ecumenical issues I referred to the preaching stole designed for me by a Carmelite nun. Its symbolic intertwining of the Celtic Cross and the Burning Bush underlines the point.

While talking of spirituality, it is relevant to make reference to one of the more bitter controversies to trouble the Church of Scotland during the last quarter of the twentieth century. At the Woman's Guild Annual Meeting in 1982 the National President, Mrs Anne Hepburn, had used a prayer of the hymn-writer Brian Wren, which included the phrases 'God our Mother' and 'Dear Mother God'. These words raised more eyebrows than supplications among Guild members and, in the General Assembly held a few weeks later, it was proposed by the Reverend James Weatherhead that the Assembly 'invite the Woman's Guild to appoint a small study group to consult with the Panel on Doctrine on the theological implications of the concept of the motherhood of God and report to a subsequent General Assembly'. A vote was forced by the Very Reverend Dr John Gray who argued that, if the Assembly wished this work to be done, it should be considered not under the report of the Woman's Guild but on the report of the Panel on Doctrine. After a brief debate Dr Weatherhead's motion carried by 390 votes to 290, indicating a house somewhat divided, to say the least.

Two years later the Report of the Woman's Guild/Panel on Doctrine Study Group appeared. As the Church had a right to expect, this was strongly grounded in Scripture and theology. It provided thoughtful insights into the language we use when we speak of and to God and offered illuminating comment on the nature of religious imagery. The report was presented to the General Assembly of 1984 in an atmosphere of some hostility, with the Moderator ruling, for example, that Mrs Hepburn did not require to respond to a question asking 'whether the Divine She is a vegetarian or does she wear a CND badge?' (Not the most incisive question I've heard in thirty years of attending General Assemblies!) There was obvious irritation at the report's assertion that people 'feel alienated and distanced from their Maker and Saviour by the exclusive use in the Church of male language for a God known not to be male'. Asked to substantiate this claim, the late Dr Alan Lewis of New College, and one of the Panel's members on the Study Group, responded by pointing to evidence gathered by the Group from interviews and submissions. He then went on to speak of the hostility with which his presentation of the report had been received a few weeks previously by the Guild Annual Meeting adding, in a telling comment:

> it was one of the saddest moments of my life to hear a plea for help, a cry of anguish from people who feel excluded from the Church being treated with derision by those who feel comfortable within the Church.[1]

However, this did not carry much weight in the Assembly either and, when it came to considering the deliverance, an amendment was moved to the traditional proposal to 'receive the report'. This asked, simply, that the Assembly should 'receive the Report, thank and discharge the Study Group and depart from the matter'. Those who spoke in favour of this approach argued, in essence, that the issue was trivial and not worthy of the Assembly's serious consideration. When put to a vote the amendment carried by a sufficiently clear majority not to require a card vote. Not, in my view, the General Assembly's finest hour! However, that was twenty years ago. Today, without apparent objection, the Church's Book of Common Order contains the prayer: 'God our father, mother, creator, protector, made in your image, we adore you.'[2]

The point of mentioning this controversy here is that it underlines the need for the Church to be open to new spiritual insights. The traditional image of God as an elderly man with a beard owes much to those portraits of Victorian divines which adorn vestries up and down the land. The reality is that for many people the image of 'God the Father' comes over not so much as the 'loving heavenly Father' of the Gospels, but more as a stern and judgemental patriarch. The supplementing of the 'father' image by other Scriptural metaphors, including the mothering one, adds to our store of spirituality and enriches our relationship with the God whose 'glory flames from star to star, centre and soul of every sphere, yet to each loving heart how near!'[3] The Church of Scotland must see itself, therefore, not only as the Church of Chalmers and Knox, Ninian and Columba, but also as the Church of Margaret and of Thanew.[4] I suggest, then, that as we move into the twenty-first century, as well as drawing on our rich historical roots, we must also be open to the renewal that comes from fresh spiritual insights. Not everything which is dismissed as 'new age' is hostile to the Gospel or unfriendly to the Church.

Then there is the matter of the Church as 'a national Church'. We have already noted that the Kirk's understanding of itself as a national Church has more to do with responsibility and service than with privilege. With an adult communicant membership of 600,000 and, according to the 2001 census, 2.1 million Scots (around 40 per cent) claiming a connection, the Church of Scotland is certainly a strong national institution. What the equivalent statistics will be in ten, or twenty years time, remains open to conjecture. Like political parties and trades unions the mainline churches are faced with a diminishing membership base. For the Church the negative impression is further emphasised by the fact that new levels of church membership were achieved in the late Victorian era, a pattern which continued until the middle of the twentieth century. Since then, statistically speaking, it has been all downhill! However, it is also widely recognised that fifty years ago social pressures made it advantageous to belong to the Church in a way it no longer does. Nowadays, failure to attend church does not indicate any lack of respectability. Quite simply, those who are active within the life of the Church are there because they have made a positive choice. Their motivation is religious rather than social. It is highly significant, for example, that though the membership statistics have declined from year to year, the Church's income, in real terms, has risen. The fact that fewer members give more speaks for itself in terms of commitment. The great question, of course, is how long this pattern will continue and it is only prudent to anticipate that it may not be for long.[5] This is what is driving proposed cutbacks in centrally funded work so that local parish work around the country can be maintained.

That said, it is important to make the point that there is much work to be done over the coming years to give a more strategic and efficient shape to the local church. It is a gross misrepresentation to allege, as is often done, that the central administration is prodigal while the local church is frugal. The General Trustees, the statutory body in which the great bulk of the Church's property is vested, reported their concern to the 2003 General Assembly 'that there is an urgent requirement that the Church reduce its liabilities in the matter of maintenance of buildings'.[6] This is undeniably the case. One of the consequences of the 1843 Disruption was a building boom in churches, church halls and manses. The reunion of 1929 resulted in a massive duplication of resources and, gradually, over the past seventy-five years, these have been rationalised. But at what price? The sad reality is that sensible efforts to unite neighbouring congregations under one roof have all too frequently led to bitter disputes, loss of membership, ministerial disillusionment and a questioning by many as to whether our true devotion is to Jesus Christ, or the Victorian buildings in which we happened to have been baptised. It is therefore imperative that presbyteries and congregations work together, as a matter of the highest priority, on a sensible planning process which will lead to the identification of those church buildings which are strategically necessary for the future witness of the Church of Scotland. These can then be given the required investment, including adaptation for contemporary needs, while the others are disposed of, with gratitude for all that they have given in their day, but without undue sentimentality or misdirected devotion. Such wise stewardship will also ensure that the Church can maintain a presence in those areas where it is not financially economic to do so, but where such a presence is called for by the continuing commitment to be a national church, exercising a territorial ministry.

Such a programme of rationalisation at local level can also facilitate the development of team ministries, such as were called for by the Committee of Forty and, more recently, by *Church without Walls* and the Board of National Mission's Task Force for Change. My own twenty-five years of parish ministry were spent in the traditional one-minister, one-congregation, one-church-building pattern. Those were good and happy days but I recognise that such a pattern is becoming increasingly uneconomic. By contrast, where two or more congregations come together in one building, at a stroke financial overheads are massively reduced. If the resulting membership were considered too large for one minister, then reduced fabric liabilities can fund an appropriate level of church staffing – minister, associate, auxiliary, youth worker, administrator, outreach worker and others as required. Church buildings would be properly maintained, attractive and welcoming – places people would want to come to! Such a dynamic presence at the heart of communities the length and breadth of the land would do much to improve the image and profile of the Kirk, enabling it to speak with greater confidence and conviction to the people of Scotland.

It is also important that the Church of Scotland should continue to speak at the national level, through comment on the great issues of the day. Sometimes the Church is accused of interfering in politics, an accusation usually levelled by politicians who do not take kindly to criticism. The fact is, however, that there is much in the Bible which indicates that God cares passionately about the kind of society in which his people live. If one of the low points of General Assemblies I have attended was the failure in 1984 to take seriously debate on the Motherhood of God report, among the high points have certainly been debates on the report of the Church and Nation Committee. For example, many will recall the late George MacLeod fulminating, through the 1960s and 1970s, and even into the 1980s, on the iniquity of nuclear weapons; yet year after year the General Assembly would endorse the traditional deterrence line. One of Lord MacLeod's fiercest opponents was an elder from Elie, the late Mr G. N. Warnock. A retired military man, Mr Warnock spoke sincerely and convincingly in those cold-war days of the need for a credible deterrent of the nuclear threat posed by others. Then came Chernobyl and that year, 1986, a different script was followed. True to form, Lord MacLeod urged that 'in our continuing witness for peace in seeking an end to the Arms Race and in re-affirming commitment to a nuclear weapons freeze, the Church's response must be clear and unequivocal'. Mr Warnock rose to his feet and from the start the Assembly sensed this was going to be different. He began: 'Moderator, I have resisted Lord MacLeod's motions on this matter year after year, but the time has come for me personally to change my stance on this.' He continued:

> We have seen through a small leakage in Russia that many countries can be affected . . . Twice in my lifetime people have been authorised to murder and to maim an enemy . . . Now, if I were – as I was in the last War, with the rank of Colonel – if I were ordered to press the button for a first nuclear strike I would not be prepared to do it. I would shoot myself first.[7]

After recording Mr Warnock's speech the verbatim record, in an understated kind of way, notes '(Applause)'. I can still hear it! It was a dramatic moment. For the record, since 1983 the General Assembly has consistently maintained 'that nuclear arms, including readiness to use them, are by their nature morally and theologically wrong'.[8]

For the Assembly to discuss such matters is not to interfere in politics. It is, rather, to bring the voice of Christian conscience and conviction to the debate on matters of great national importance. And while I have highlighted nuclear weapons, there are many aspects of public life – education, social policy, law reform, charity regulation, health care – on which the Church of Scotland is invited by government agencies to make comment and regularly does so. The establishment of a Scottish Parliamentary Office was a timely ecumenical initiative by the Kirk and provides a well-used channel for informed engagement between churches and the Scottish Parliament.

The Church of Scotland must also retain its global perspective. We have seen how throughout its long history Scottish Christianity has drawn from and contributed to the faith in all the world. Scots have, traditionally, been great travellers and have taken their religion and their culture wherever they have gone. While, as we saw in Chapter 3 the nature of the Church's overseas engagement has changed, it still remains an important part of what the Kirk is, finding expression, no less, in the first of the Articles Declaratory. This Article, which sets the tone for all the rest, underlines the fact that our calling as the Church of Scotland continues to involve 'labouring for the advancement of the Kingdom of God throughout the world'.

It is clear that in these early years of the new century the Church is having to go through a process of cutting its coat according to its cloth. The 2004 General Assembly will have to take tough decisions on prioritising areas of work which are carried out centrally. Congregations, as ever, will also be seeking to maintain a balance between funding local parish work and contributing to the wider mission of the Church, in Scotland and beyond. In such circumstances it might appear tempting simply to cut back on work beyond Scotland altogether and concentrate on 'keeping the home fires burning'. My own sense is that such a policy would fundamentally alter the nature of the Church of Scotland. I am not saying that work beyond Scotland should be exempt from budget cuts; simply, that it should not be regarded as peripheral and easily dispensed with. I recall a conversation with a fellow former Moderator on this very subject. We both agreed how good it would have been if we could have taken all the members of the Church of Scotland on overseas visits to some of the world's poorest people. Not only would they have had their hearts touched and eyes opened, as we did. They would also have witnessed at first hand the high value attached by Christian people around the world to their relationship with the Kirk.

Finally, under this section I mention again the question, 'What does the Church of Scotland believe?' One substantial piece of unfinished business from the last century concerns the Westminster Confession of Faith. As we saw, the General Assembly of 1974 came close to altering its status from 'subordinate standard' to 'historic statement' but, at the last minute, drew back, pending the preparation of a new Statement of Faith. While the Word of God, contained in the Scriptures of the Old and New Testaments, remains the supreme standard of faith and life it is less than satisfactory that the second most important repository of official church doctrine should continue to be a document from the seventeenth century, adherence to which is so hedged about with qualifications. It would be a fine thing indeed were a new Confession to be drawn up which set out the substance of the faith in clear and contemporary language. Such a document could do much to boost the Church's confidence as it moves into the twenty-first century. People asking the question, 'What does the Church of Scotland believe?' could be handed a straightforward document in everyday language, rather than being given a complicated explanation involving Creeds, Confessions and Declaratory Acts. As we have seen, much work in this area was done in the late 1960s and early 1970s and could readily be revisited. Certainly we have the 1992 Statement, printed as an Appendix to Chapter 10 above, and this provides a useful teaching tool for new members and for those taking on responsibilities such as the eldership. However, as was made clear when it was approved, this was not in any way purporting to be a new and official Confession of Faith.

THE ECUMENICAL AND INTER-FAITH AGENDA

At time of writing the dust has not yet settled following the decision of the 2003 General Assembly to depart from the SCIFU process.[9] It is therefore too early to predict where the next ecumenical initiatives will lie. It is certainly to be expected that the Church of Scotland will continue to play a leading role in the various national and international bodies such as Action of Churches Together in Scotland (ACTS), Churches Together in Britain and Ireland (CTBI), the World Alliance of Reformed Churches (WARC), the Conference of European Churches (CEC) and the World Council of Churches (WCC). There is also an increasing recognition within the Church that it makes sense to act, both locally and nationally, with other churches wherever that is possible. A very obvious example is Christian Aid Week, already well established in communities across Scotland as a shared endeavour. More and more 'Churches Together' groups are being established to undertake local initiatives and this is much to be encouraged. After SCIFU it is not so easy to foresee any imminent moves towards structural union involving the Church of Scotland, though the day for such a thing will no doubt come again. The immediately obvious contender would be the United Free Church, should that Church feel that its concerns over Church-and-State issues, which kept it out of the 1929 union, have been allayed. Beyond that, though I dare say further down the road, there is our historic co-heir to the Scottish Reformation tradition, the Scottish Episcopal Church. Having struggled to live together in the one Kirk for 130 years Presbyterians and Episcopalians went their separate ways in 1690. Whether we can come back together, in the manner of uniting churches around the world, remains to be seen.

In this ecumenical context another interesting General Assembly controversy comes to mind. In 1979 the General Assembly approved a proposal that the Chair of Christian Dogmatics at Edinburgh University be renamed the Thomas Chalmers Chair in Theology. During the course of the Assembly a rumour began to circulate that the first holder of this chair was to be a Roman Catholic theologian, James P. Mackey, Professor of Systematic and Philosophical Theology at the University of San Francisco. There was no doubting Professor Mackey's academic qualifications for the job, but the question being raised was whether it was appropriate for a Catholic theologian to be responsible for teaching large numbers of students for the ministry of the Church of Scotland. In terms of a concordat between the Church and the University such appointments were made by a joint committee of both and, as the rumours grew and the story was reported in the press, the Assembly took the unusual step of recalling the Convener of the Board of Nomination to Church Chairs. Questions of confidentiality and accountability arose and there were many points of order and interventions by the Procurator. No names were mentioned but, at the end of the day, the Assembly was presented with a motion by the Very Reverend Dr John Gray asking that, if the rumoured nomination proceeded, 'the General Assembly request the Court not to ratify the appointment, if that course be open to them, but to direct that the Chair be re-advertised'. Against this another former Moderator from the Presbytery of Stirling and

Dunblane, and regular sparring partner of Dr Gray, the Very Reverend Dr Peter Brodie, moved that 'the General Assembly put their trust in their representatives on the Board of Nomination to Church Chairs and respect their argument for the need to preserve confidentiality under the present regulations'. When the vote was taken Dr Gray's motion carried by 412 votes to 254. The Moderator, Professor Robin Barbour, could not resist observing with waspish amusement: 'Having done a very rapid sum I note that the total number of votes cast was 666.'[10] It is a measure of how far things have come ecumenically that it is difficult to envisage the same controversy arising today, certainly to the same extent. The debate reflected a harking back to the days when the great majority of teachers in University Divinity Faculties were ministers of the Church of Scotland who had had parish experience. Indeed that point was made quite specifically with a deliverance passed, before the rumours started, noting 'with concern' that this was no longer the case. For the record, Professor Mackey was duly appointed to the Chair and the University of Edinburgh issued a statement reassuring the Church of Scotland and acknowledging its obligation to provide academic training for the Church's students for the ministry.

On the inter-faith front there is great potential for continuing dialogue and developing relations. It will be apparent from the chapter devoted to this topic that much of the interaction to date has been among the leadership of faith communities. I wonder whether there are parallels with the ecumenical process. When I was growing up in Dundee I used to play with the sons of a neighbouring Roman Catholic family. This was a great novelty and I can remember some consternation when I asked my parents if I could go to Confession with Brian and Derek. This didn't happen, but my 'pals' did take me into their church one day, pointing out the Stations of the Cross and showing me what to do with the holy water. I remember being disappointed that I couldn't return the compliment because our church was locked during the week. In those days, half a century ago, the prospect of a priest and a minister having a pulpit exchange was unthinkable, yet, thanks to initiatives such as the Week of Prayer for Christian Unity and united Holy Week services, it is not at all uncommon for Catholics and Protestants to worship in each other's churches. Will similar developments follow in terms of inter-faith relations? Clearly there are differences. Protestants and Catholics are both Christian and can therefore worship together with integrity. The same is not true of members of a Church of Scotland congregation and a neighbouring mosque. And yet, if relationships are to develop across faith boundaries, there has to be dialogue and engagement, not just between minister and imam, but also involving the members of both communities. The prospect of pulpit exchanges across faith boundaries may sound fanciful, but if confined to an exchange of greetings and courtesies, is it entirely out of the question? After all, integrity is hardly compromised by extending the hand of friendship. As recorded in Chapter 8 I have actually had that experience, though it was in Syria, not Scotland.

GOVERNMENT AND LEADERSHIP

I speculated in the previous section about future ecumenical developments and noted the historical legacy of the Scottish Reformation shared by both the Kirk and the Scottish Episcopal Church. Will these two traditions ever come together again in a 1929-style reunion? The big issue for the Kirk, of course, is bishops and, as SCIFU showed, notwithstanding Episcopal clarification of the nature of the office, historic anxieties remain real for many within the Church of Scotland. Given that, as previously noted, part of the function of the bishop in an Episcopal church is to offer leadership, the question remains as to how leadership is exercised within a Presbyterian church. The Church of England can say: 'Synodical government and Episcopal leadership'. The Church of Scotland can only say: 'Presbyterian government'.

We touched on these questions in Chapter 4. There is no denying the integrity and credibility which underpin Presbyterian principles of a hierarchy of courts rather than of individuals, parity of ministers and collegiality within the courts of the church among ministers, elders and deacons. The recognition of Christ as King and Head of the Church, and the affirming of the doctrine of the priesthood of all believers, provides a well-grounded theological basis for the life of the church. Nor can it be argued that such a system is, in principle, anti-leadership. The fact is that, within such a framework, those with gifts of leadership can and do emerge, influencing debates and decisions within the courts of the Church, convening committees of the General Assembly and, perhaps, being recognised within the wider counsels of the nation's life. Scottish ecclesiastical and civil history can testify to many such individuals.

While all of this is true, there is another argument, based largely on the question of media profile. This argument has grown louder in recent years and often centres on the question of whether the Moderator of the General Assembly should serve for a longer period than one year. I will not rehearse the points outlined in Chapter 4, but I do have a sense that the argument will grow more forceful in the coming years. I also suggest that it is this kind of 'recognition' question which may eventually lead to a fresh examination of the vexed question of 'bishops in the Kirk'. The simple fact is that, were you to stop ten people in Princes Street or Sauchiehall Street on a Saturday afternoon and ask them what a bishop was, most would be able to tell you. Ask them what a moderator was and I guess you would get a lot of blank expressions. Now this may sound trivial, but it does make a serious point about communication. Accordingly, the argument that might develop would be to offer the Church a choice. This choice would be: either to stick with the present policy on leadership and go largely ignored by the wider community; or recognise that the medium of communication most likely to be heard and noticed is an identifiable leader whom people can get to know over a period of time. I have already observed, based on experience, that a moderatorial statement is more likely to attract a headline than a comment by a convener, still less by a committee. If this kind of pressure leads eventually towards a longer term of office for the Moderator, then, as I have argued in Chapter 4, the Moderator of the General Assembly will inevitably accrue a national leadership role. In time a similar development may well arise at presbytery level, and then we will have full-time national and regional leaders. If that day comes then, effectively, we will have bishops. I am not saying this will happen, but I can certainly see how it could happen.

I am, however, certain that any such developments would take place within the structure of church courts. Accordingly, the General Assembly will continue to evolve in its hybrid role of church parliament and party conference. Though not commanding the television coverage it once did the annual General Assembly remains a significant event in the life of Scotland and attracts a level of media coverage envied by many delegates from churches overseas. In the 1997 reforms the membership of the Assembly was reduced from around 1,100 to 850. Financial pressures over the coming years may lead to a further reduction, though such a reduction would obviously mean individual ministers, elders and deacons attending less frequently. Continuing work also needs to be done to ensure the right balance between conducting the business of the Assembly, decently and in order, and creating a gathering which is celebratory and inspirational. I believe that the Board of Practice and Procedure's 1996 comment that 'the Church looks annually to the General Assembly for something hard to define, yet real in terms of identity'[11] remains valid. If savings need to be made my vote would be for a smaller Assembly meeting annually rather than a larger one meeting every two or three years. Presbyteries, too, will continue to develop. The streamlining of vacancy procedures by giving powers to routine decision making to a committee may well offer a model for other areas with full meetings of the court occurring less frequently and being devoted to more substantial matters of regional strategy and policy.

CONCLUSION

As I stated in the Introduction, my purpose in writing this book was threefold. It was, in part, to show that the Church can take pride in the way it has changed and developed over the years. It has not always covered itself in glory, but there have been brave initiatives and progressive decisions which can give us cause for confidence. I have tried also to show that the culture of change through which we are presently living is by no means a new thing. Rather change is of the very essence of the Gospel and is thus integral to the life of a church which is faithful to the Gospel. Finally, I have sought to share something of my own overview of significant moments in the life of the Church of Scotland during a ministry which has covered the last three decades. It will be for others to judge the degree of success with which I have achieved these aims but my hope is that some, at least, of those who read will find renewed confidence in a changing Church and a revitalised faith in the Gospel.

NOTES

1 Verbatim Record, General Assembly, 1984, p. 548.
2 *Common Order*, 1994, p. 446.
3 *CH3*, Hymn 34, 'Lord of all being throned afar' (Oliver Wendell Holmes).
4 Mother of St Mungo.
5 By way of illustration the Board of Stewardship and Finance projected an increase in Ordinary General Income of just 2 per cent in 2004, compared with a 2.5 per cent increase the previous year. See Supplementary Report to the General Assembly, 2003, section 6.3.
6 Reports to the General Assembly, 2003, p. 3/10.
7 Verbatim Record, General Assembly, 1986, p. 737.
8 Deliverance of the General Assembly on the Report of the Church and Nation Committee, 1983, section 23.
9 See Chapter 7.
10 See Revelation 13:18.
11 See Chapter 4.

Index of People

Index of Subjects

209